Pynchon: The Voice of Ambiguity

Pynchon: The Voice of Ambiguity

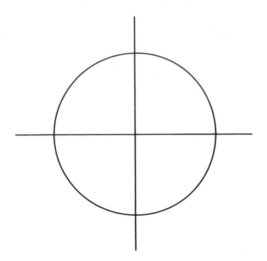

Thomas H. Schaub

University of Illinois Press

Urbana   Chicago   London

The author gratefully acknowledges the following for quoted
material from the works of Thomas Pynchon:

The Crying of Lot 49, copyright 1966 by Thomas Pynchon,
Harper & Row, Publishers, Inc.

"Entropy," copyright 1960 by Kenyon College.

Gravity's Rainbow, copyright 1973 by Thomas Pynchon, Viking Penguin Inc.

"Under the Rose," copyright 1961 by the World Publishing
Company.

V., copyright 1963 by Thomas Pynchon, Harper & Row, Publishers, Inc.

Library of Congress Cataloging in Publication Data

Schaub, Thomas H   1947–
  Pynchon: The Voice of Ambiguity

  Bibliography: p.
  Includes index.
  1. Pynchon, Thomas—Criticism and interpretation.
I. Title.
PS3566.Y55Z87   813'.54   80–11944
ISBN 0–252–00816–2

To my Mother and Father,
who shared in the work

Contents

Preface   ix

ONE
Pynchon's Project: Fiction in Four Dimensions   3

TWO
The Crying of Lot 49: "A Gentle Chill, an Ambiguity"   21

THREE
Pynchon's Great Song   43

FOUR
History and Fiction: From Providence to Paranoia   76

FIVE
Reading Pynchon   103

SIX
Pynchon's Company   139

Bibliography   155

Index   161

Preface

I chose to study the writing of Thomas Pynchon because my friend Phil Russ was so enthusiastic about *Gravity's Rainbow*. I first read the book in 1974, and for me it still remains one of the persistent encounters of my intellectual life. My initial efforts at understanding this massive book were characterized by a frustrating search for repetition, symmetry, and a consistency revealing Pynchon's true disposition and theme. The experience of reading Pynchon, however, is really an analogue of the conundrums of search his books describe, for they depend upon the tyrannizing desire of the mind for unity and meaning.

The uncertainties and ambiguities which attend the reading of Pynchon's fiction are not a failure of the reader nor a result of authorial neglect or confusion. Pynchon's scrupulousness is amply manifest in *The Crying of Lot 49*, where ambiguity is most visibly the result of an intentional stylistic strategy. Pynchon's concern with ambiguity may be located in the representative complaint of Sidney Stencil, the aging diplomat of his first novel *V.*, who believed that "we carry on the business of this century with an intolerable double vision." From the early story "Entropy" to *Gravity's Rainbow*, Pynchon's primary purpose has been to dramatize twentieth-century extremism and with it the loss of any temperate balance.

This book is about Pynchon's stylistic balance between the poles of the "intolerable double vision" presented in his fiction. The experience of ambiguity in the reading of Pynchon is essential. It is a necessary result of his design to bring readers to the uncertainties of the precarious balance where possibilities abound, where the familiar is strange, where the benign is evil, and where the rage for order is persistently denied. This is the effect of reading Pynchon. It may well be his most distinctive achievement as a writer, for the careful asymmetry of his unresolved oppositions enforces a rare balance—opens a still difficult middle ground—between the nightmarish extremes that claim our allegiance.

A gratifying reward of writing this book has been the community of Pynchon's readers it has given me. I want especially to thank two of its members: Khachig Tölölyan, whose work nurtures a growing number of informed readers and critics of Pynchon; and Edward Mendelson, the critic I found most useful in developing my own thoughts, whose kindness and intellectual support I greatly appreciate. I would also like to acknowledge Phil Russ, again, for reading and editing some of the manuscript; Jeff Ebinger and Jeff Bartlett, for hours of critical discussion and for listening; Ed Folsom and Wayne Franklin of the Department of English of the University of Iowa for reading the manuscript; the University of Iowa library, for its many services; Bonnie Depp for her able copyediting; and the University of Illinois Press staff, particularly Harriet Stockanes, for their assistance and patience.

My special gratitude to Sherman Paul, who has been unfailingly helpful and kind as a friend, encouraging and thorough as a mentor. He has read and edited the manuscript in its many revisions; my requests for assistance in matters of style and accuracy of expression have been granted without hesitation. In these last months of preparation, the warm enthusiasm both Sherman and his wife, Jim, have shown me has been more than I deserve.

The physical grace to keep working has been generously given me by many, including those I have mentioned, but first among them my parents.

T. H. S.

Iowa City, 1980

It's a long walk home tonight.
Listen to this mock-angel singing,
let your communion be at least in
listening, even if they are not
spokesmen for your exact hopes,
your exact, darkest terror, listen.

One

Pynchon's Project:
Fiction in Four Dimensions

> There is nothing unscientific in the
> idea that, beyond the lines of force
> felt by the senses, the universe
> may be—as it has always been—
> either a supersensuous chaos or
> a divine unity, which irresistibly
> attracts, and is either life or death
> to penetrate.
>
> Henry Adams, *The Education of Henry Adams*

In Thomas Pynchon's writing uncertainty is a condition of our experience in the world. The modern origin of this view lies in the erosion of nineteenth-century optimism and the developments of twentieth-century science and politics, a turning point that has its dramatic literary expression in the autobiography of Henry Adams. Writing in 1905, Adams already requires the stylistic self-consciousness that comes to characterize modernist posture. His *Education* remains contemporary for us because of its delicate ironies; but as with Pynchon, the self-conscious style expresses a relation to a world in which the confidence of unity has been suddenly replaced by a bewildering "multiplicity."

Like Adams, Pynchon seeks a form of expression that conforms to the lack of formal certainties in the world he is describing. This underlies the primary effect of Pynchon's writing. The reader experiences Pynchon's fiction as representative of a determinate order which it suggests but which it persistently withholds. This quality—this impenetrableness—is intensified by the ways in which Pynchon encourages the reader to suspect that this withheld order is so withheld only by remaining unnamed; that a revelatory unity is present in the text, but without confirmation or recognition. Pynchon's books, accordingly, establish for the reader an intentional and strict uncertainty, for they repeat in our relation to them the conditional relation to the world which Adams's either/or logic so clearly expresses.

This book is a study of the ideas and techniques by which Pynchon achieves the uneasy poise conjured by such logic. That poise is the defining characteristic of the fiction he writes and of our uncertain relation to the worlds his fiction intends. Pynchon may be said to write from both "sides" of the ridge Adams's logic creates, because his fiction aspires to the condition of simultaneity, in which contradictory possibilities co-exist. In his development toward a simultaneous fiction, Pynchon exploits the curious relations of our familiar three-dimensional world to the four-dimensional world that encloses it. In his books, the time-bound world of the senses is suffused with the four-dimensional world of the space-time continuum. The four-dimensional world is used by Pynchon as the scientific expression of continuity unavailable to us on "this side," and is a figure for the continuities of timeless meaning and connection which exist at once with the historical time his characters and readers experience. This "beyond" is invoked not as indication of an alternative reality permitting escape from our condition, but as part of Pynchon's project to establish the poise between fragmentary experience and continuous meaning. Such continuity is never a release from doubt but is an intensifying of the importance of that uncertainty. Pynchon's stylistic balancing orders the ideas and visions of his fiction so that they remain, as they do for Adams, strict and luminous possibilities rather than mere facts, animating clues instead of answers.

This introductory chapter provides an overview of these determining ideas and intentions. Specific exegesis of his books is reserved until this groundwork has been laid; the last chapter, "Reading Pynchon," describes the stylistic strategy which creates the ambiguity confronting the reader and traces Pynchon's development from a writer of narrative prose to a speaker of oratory and singer of song, as he puts aside the guise of disinterested author and speaks directly to his audience in the great song of *Gravity's Rainbow*.

The reflections of Sidney Stencil, a character in Pynchon's first novel, *V.*, are a paradigm of the uncertainties which confound both the characters and the readers of Pynchon's writing. In the days prior to his death Stencil wrote in his journal, "'Short of examining the entire history of each individual participating, . . . short of anatomizing each soul, what hope has anyone of understanding a Situation?'" (443). For the elder Stencil, his theory of the Situation is a way of explaining the difficulties faced in his diplomatic profession, but it is a theory which Stencil himself abstracts into a philosophical idea that applies equally well to Pynchon's writing, for his project is the creation of fictional Situations as complex and uncertain for the reader as they are for the characters within them.

The principal idea informing the Situations of Pynchon's writing is the ominous fact expressed by Norbert Wiener that "the universe is running downhill."[1] Entropy is a measure of that decline. Pynchon's indebtedness to Wiener is visible in his short story "Entropy,"[2] where the character Callisto's choice of words and the order of his argument repeat Wiener's discussion of entropy in *The Human Use of Human Beings*. Pynchon's use of entropy as a metaphor of decline underlies all of his fiction. The law of entropy obtains only under certain conditions, however; Pynchon's use of the concept shows that he is more concerned with the ways in which his characters respond to the threat of decline than with the fact of decline itself.

Wiener discusses at length the human response to entropy and the retarding or "saving" possibilities which feedback affords. These possibilities are elements of renewal in the Situations Pynchon creates, and take the form of sacred intervention, secular meaning and information, subversive social groups, and suggestions of a sentient universe. These elements are also presented under the aspect of the entropy metaphor, for they represent in Pynchon's novels the generative sources of what Wiener has called the "enclaves of life"—a phrase Pynchon borrows from *The Human Use of Human Beings* and uses in "Entropy."

"Entropy" begins with a quotation often cited as evidence of Pynchon's blackness: "We must get into step, a lockstep toward the prison of death. There is no escape. The weather will not change." But these words from Henry Miller's *Tropic of Cancer* are followed a few sentences later by this paradox: "I have no money, no resources, no hopes. I am the happiest man alive."[3] The fact of decline and eventual death is hardly arguable, but the human response to this fact is at issue in both Miller and Pynchon, and is the key to Pynchon's writing, for it is nothing less than the relation between what we call "life" and the larger processes of which it is a part.

In Pynchon's writing the imminence of death and the chances of a vital alternative are always set in opposition to one another. This has given rise to the conclusion that Pynchon's writings are either relentlessly pessimistic or that his "salad of despair" (CL49, 5) is seasoned with a carefully disguised spice of hope, which takes the form of timeless myth, mystic egolessness, and other species of anti-rational Oneness. But this opposition and its proliferation throughout his fictional situations are themselves typical of the world "in a West of such extremes" (V., 440), and are used by Pynchon as a structuring device and theme to characterize the increasingly polarized Situation in which modern western man finds himself. The primary figures of his fiction are always caught between these poles, and experience the alienation and ambiguity which accompany their lives in the "excluded middle" (CL49, 136).

Entropy may be defined briefly here as a measure of disorder within closed systems, a disorder characterized by the redistribution of a system's parts into the more probable randomness of disorganization. The social and political expression of this disorder was first proposed by Henry Adams[4] and appears early in Pynchon's writing (which refers to Adams) in the short stories "Lowlands," "Entropy," and "Under the Rose."[5] The themes of "Under the Rose" are developed in the Stencil Sr. subplot of V., where the process of decay is demonstrated by the loss of nineteenth-century civilities ("The Situation used to be a civilized affair," Sidney Stencil complains, V., 456) and the takeover of politics by "amateurs" in the street (461). Stencil's despair over this proliferation of plots and designs that derive from no careful agreement among discreet knowns is a political expression of that general loss of clarity associated with the close of the century which is a commonplace of intellectual history, and which includes the alterations of Newton's conception of the universe, as Wiener explains: "Newtonian physics, which had ruled from the end of the seventeenth century to the end of the nineteenth with scarcely an opposing voice, described a universe in which everything happened precisely according to law, a compact, tightly organized universe in which the whole future depends strictly upon the whole past." The popular "clockwork" perception of the Newtonian view assumed the possibility of precise measurements to supply the "initial positions and momenta" of systems to which Newton's physical laws apply, but this accuracy is not, in fact, attainable, and the methodology of physics has incorporated the "science of distribution" to accommodate the ineradicable imprecision. The activity of atomic and planetary worlds (and what we can expect or predict about them) is more accurately described statistically: "The functional part of physics, in other words, cannot escape considering uncertainty and the contingency of events."[6]

It is not difficult to see evidence of this "contingency" in Pynchon's fictional Situations. In them uncertainty is a condition of their structure: the problems his characters face have less to do with solipsism than with trying to live in a Situation whose history has been shaped by forces inimical to humane interests. These have replicated beyond anyone's ability to understand them, and their random interaction has created a contingent tissue of events intended by no single force or group.

The bizarre slapstick of V.'s chapter seven ("She Hangs on the Western Wall"), for example, is a Situation in which four distinct plots intersect only because they share an initial (Vheissu, Venezuela, Victoria, and the "Birth of Venus"); this accidental intersection results in the very real crescendo of violence which closes that chapter. Similarly, when the narrator of Gravity's Rainbow tells us "this is how they meet" (365), it is not until twenty-eight pages later—after Tyrone stumbles on Säure and Magda, is christened Rocketman, infiltrates the Potsdam conference, is kidnapped by Tchitcherine, and is left to awake in a Neubabelsberg movie studio—that Tyrone and Greta do meet (393), and what intervenes is hardly the cause and effect of premeditated design— though cause and effect it is.

Both these examples demonstrate Pynchon's intention to mirror in his fiction a world Situation in which accident is not separate from design but is the passive result of many designs operating at cross-purposes to each other. This is a significant fact for readers of Pynchon's books, for the clarity of individual plot strands and isolated narrative commentary leads readers to assume a final coherence of elements and that the whole may be described from the vantage of that coherence. But Pynchon's writing does not yield to a deterministic analysis, in which each novelistic element is linked in a grand narrative chain of cause and effect. This is not to say that Pynchon disregards cause and effect; only that, as in physics, cause and effect is a limited model of prediction, of how things work. Events do influence one another, but the resulting pattern of effects will be described differently, as Einstein has shown, by observers located in different places. This cliché of relativity is the basis of Stencil's theory: "no Situation had any objective reality: it only existed in the minds of those who happened to be in on it at any specific moment. Since these several minds tended to form a sum total or complex more mongrel than homogenous, The Situation must necessarily appear to a single observer much like a diagram in four dimensions to an eye conditioned to seeing its world in only three" (V., 174).

Readers have pointed to the narrator's tired and condescending "You will want cause and effect. All right" (GR, 663) as proof of Pynchon's rejection of that relation, but his disdain derives from the fact that as author he is able to transcend the more narrow cause-and-effect world and write in the fourth dimension of time unavailable to Sidney Stencil. This is a crucial point, for the relation between the worlds of four and three dimensions is analogous to the relation discussed above between the larger processes of the universe and the more narrow experience we call "life." Writing in 1921, Arthur Eddington addresses directly the issue raised by the spatiality of the fourth dimension in his book *Space, Time and Gravitation: An Outline of the General Relativity Theory*. The following passages are taken from chapter III, "The World of Four Dimensions":

The division into past and future (a feature of time-order which has no analogy in space-order) is closely associated with our ideas of causation and free-will. In a perfectly determinate scheme the past and future may

be regarded as lying mapped out—as much available to present exploration as the distant parts of space. Events do not happen; they are just
there, and we come across them. 'The formality of taking place' is merely
the indication that the observer has on his voyage of exploration passed
into the absolute future of the event in question; and it has no important
significance. We can be aware of an eclipse in the year 1999, very much as
we are aware of an unseen companion to Algol. Our knowledge of things
where we are not, and of things *when* we are not, is essentially the
same—an inference (sometimes a mistaken inference) from brain im-
pressions, including memory, *here* and *now*.

Eddington's comments are very like scientific support for the old
Boethean explanation of God's omniscience and man's free will.
Like Boethius, Eddington offers this caveat:

But that statement that time is a fourth dimension may suggest unnec-
essary difficulties which a more precise definition avoids. It is in the
external world that the four dimensions are united—not in the relations
of the external world to the individual which constitute his direct ac-
quaintance with space and time. Just in that process of relation to an
individual, the order falls apart into the distinct manifestations of space
and time.[7]

Pynchon's characters live between the three-dimensional world
constructed about them and the four-dimensional world they
construe; both are real, but one is experienced while the other—
like Stencil's "theory"—is an abstraction that subsumes the
three-dimensional world without abridging its laws for those
within it.

Stencil's theory gives him the solace of an explanation but does
little to diminish the chaos he sees around him. As the Maltese
Situation, reminiscent of Florence, becomes increasingly irra-
tional, Stencil muses: "The inert universe may have a quality we
can call logic. But logic is a human attribute after all; so even at
that it's a misnomer. What are real are the cross-purposes. We've
dignified them with the words 'profession' and 'occupation.'
There is a certain cold comfort in remembering that Manganese,
Mizzi, Maijstral, Dupiro the ragman, that blasted face who caught
us at the villa—also work at cross-purposes" (V., 455). These
"cross-purposes" are the political expression of the four-dimensional world which transcends the reality of any particular point
of view.

Within his novels, of course, Pynchon is the creator of those cross-purposes, and is able to insist upon the realities of the whole and its parts at the same time. He does this, moreover, without ever allowing us an adequate picture of the whole, for it remains a continuity only experienced in what the characters suspect about it; these suspicions are as much a source of confusion to them and the reader as they are the basis for meaningfulness. As Stencil's reflection demonstrates, Pynchon's Situations always establish a continuity between the material universe and social reality. This continuity has its origin in the thermodynamic metaphor discussed earlier, and it is given more emphasis in *Gravity's Rainbow*, where the molecular world has the power of speech. But even in *V.* Stencil Sr. realizes that "any Situation takes shape from events much lower than the merely human" (455). This recognition recurs in Walter Rathenau's parlor wisdom (*GR*, 165–67), and reappears in its social aspect as a form of advice from Bodine to Tyrone: "Everything is some kind of a plot, man" (603). As above, the very magnitude of the confusion provides a salutary possibility: "this network of all plots may yet carry him to freedom."

The continua which science presses upon our imaginations throw into question the place of value in the "external world," but they do so in a curious way, for the determinism which Eddington's space-time map implies is nothing we experience in our historical freedom. This distinction is important for any reading of Pynchon's fiction, for within his Situations both realms are engaged. The determinism of the behavioral plot exercised upon Tyrone is a determinism of this world which he may escape by putting in the clutch (207). In his world, distinct from the "external world," the value of his freedom is affirmed, but at the same time that Pynchon's writing supports such values it forces upon us the perspective of the larger ahistorical view which throws into doubt the entire notion of a history in which "life" has any more significance than "decay."

Pynchon's technical expertise in creating this dissonance is visible in the structure of *V.* Each episode is presented in the time-bound world of three dimensions, but these episodes are ordered nonserially in an approximation of space, so that "past" and "future" become relative terms, as they would be in a four-dimensional scheme. The present of Benny Profane is Sidney Stencil's future, and Stencil's present is history to his son, Herbert; to each his own time is "the present." The last chapter of *V.*, "Epilogue, 1919," occurs thirty-seven years "before" the chapter which precedes it, and serves to conclude the book ironically by providing an exposition that anticipates the dwindling reserves of the next generation. All history, in this sense, is a lesson to the present, but the spatialization of narrative time is one of Pynchon's techniques which underlines V.'s omnipresence and the way in which V. as a concept transcends one-way time. V. is the space-time continuum of the novel, and her appearances inside each time-bound episode are clues to a continuity outside of history.

Sidney Stencil, inside of time, records a prediction in his journal that is borne out by characters in episodes which occur elsewhere in the book's space-time:

"If there is any political moral to be found in this world . . . it is that we carry on the business of this century with an intolerable double vision. Right and Left; the hothouse and the street. The Right can only live and work hermetically, in the hothouse of the past, while outside the Left prosecute their affairs in the streets by manipulated mob violence. And cannot live but in the dreamscape of the future.

"What of the real present, the men-of-no-politics, the once-respectable Golden Mean? Obsolete; in any case, lost sight of. In a West of such extremes we can expect, at the very least, a highly 'alienated' populace within not many more years." (440)

Readers may have some confidence in the normative value of this moral, for Stencil's abstracted opposition is one that permeates not only the novel *V.* (where it recurs in the speech and thoughts of characters widely distributed) but Pynchon's other books as well; it is an opposition which corresponds to the Inside (safe, hermetic) / Outside (dangerous, street violence) dichotomy that is more visible in *The Crying of Lot 49* and *Gravity's Rainbow*. Oedipa Maas manages to be "relevant" to America only as "an alien"—making good Stencil's prediction. Like him, she is disturbed by the disappearance of the "real present" and is paralyzed by the polar extremes of her culture which excludes the middle ground she occupies. Nor is such authorial point reserved for a selected elite of characters. Early in *V.* the plastic surgeon Schoenmaker abstracts a theory similar to Stencil's moral: "correction—along all dimensions: social, political, emotional—entails retreat to a diametric opposite rather than any reasonable search for a golden mean" (91).

The "real present" is the proper relation to the extremes of the Situation this introduction has been describing. This relation is not the absolute present refuted by relativity, but is a switching point in local time in which the participant remains poised at the personal nexus of the Situation's dimensions, rejecting the violent simplicity of a swing toward any single one, and integrating their competing claims in the interest of an equilibrium both expeditious and true. Stencil's lament criticizes the extremism of our century, which seems to have lost the ability to operate at this difficult "interface." At the time we read his moral, Stencil's strength, too, is waning. In his final effort to deal with the bewildering complexity of the Maltese Situation, he summons a "last burst of duplicity and virtù" to force him "into the real present" (461). The words "duplicity" and "virtù" derive from Machiavelli's *The Prince,* especially chapter twenty-five, in which he declares that "human affairs" are "governed" by the twin forces of "fortune" or chance and "virtù"—the strength of human initiative.[8] As such, the words are confirmation of what Stencil already knows, that like Machiavelli's scheme he is obsolete. "The Situation is always bigger than you, Sidney," he reflects. "It has like God its own logic and its own justification for being, and the best you can do is cope" (455).

The "real present" remains in Pynchon's fiction that important intersection—impasse, one might say—where the dimensions of a Situation meet. It is, as we shall see with Oedipa Maas, the "excluded middle" that is the relation between what she inherits and the possible meaningfulness of that inheritance. It is a point of ambiguity and uncertainty, and to exist there, forging a path which resists extremes while integrating them into the complex truth of a Situation, is hard work. Stencil's moral occurs within a single episode, but it is one implicit in the book's structure, which forces the reader to hold at once the extremes of time and space in the "real present" of reading.

The burdens of comprehending the Situation are borne in *V.* and *The Crying of Lot 49* by a few characters (Sidney and Herbert, Old Godolphin, Oedipa), and by an enlarged cast of seekers and philosophers in *Gravity's Rainbow*, but in this last book the narrative voice clearly emerges as the consciousness trying to integrate the fragments of his world while keeping them distinct enough to remain intelligible to his listeners: "Well, there is the heart of it: the monumental yellow structure, out there in the slum-suburban night, the never-sleeping percolation of life and enterprise through its shell, Outside and Inside interpiercing one another too fast, too finely labyrinthine, for either category to have much hegemony any more. The nonstop revue crosses its stage, crowding and thinning, surprising and jerking tears in an endless ratchet" (681). These are the introductory words to the closing, nonserial sections of *Gravity's Rainbow*, and they underline one of the book's central metaphors, "it's all theatre" (3). But this is an old idea of Pynchon's whose origins are traceable to the novel *V.*, where Sidney Stencil, "old soft-shoe artist," walks the Strada Stretta: "Such were the topological deformities of this street that one seemed to walk through a succession of music-hall stages, each demarcated by a curve or slope, each with a different set and acting company but all for the same low entertainment" (440–41). An image in *V.* becomes a technique in *Gravity's Rainbow*; Stencil, viewing the congested street as theatre, becomes Pynchon, authorial witness of his own four-dimensional vision.

Not a few readers have complained that the "nonstop revue" is unintelligible,[9] but Pynchon runs the risk as part of his project to establish a fictional Situation commensurate with the reality we experience, a reality we experience in three dimensions and know in four. For the most part, even in *Gravity's Rainbow* Pynchon remains within the bounds of conventional story-telling, which observe the familiar flow of time. A fiction which came to us entirely from the Other Side not only would have to be written by someone "there" but would be fiction-all-at-once, completely unintelligible to us on This Side, as the narrator following Slothrop in his sylvan hideout knows: "no serial time over there: events are all there in the same eternal moment and so certain messages don't always 'make sense' back here: they lack historical structure, they sound fanciful, or insane" (624). Pynchon remains on this side not only because he must, in order to communicate at all, but because his nonseriality (like the structure of *V.*) is only an approximation of the "eternal moment." Such approximations are the narrative equivalents of the timelessness forming the fourth dimension of the characters' situations; like the other three (the spatial present conjured in the human relation to the fourth), it is an additional and complicating factor with which characters and readers have to contend in the "here" and "now."

The sticking point of such Situations is that the characters must have some way of living within them. All of the thoughtful and active characters manage to do so by arriving at an understanding of the Situation, of which Sidney Stencil's abstraction is the example we have been using. In one way or another, this involves for all of them the abstraction of their understanding into a concept, and this conceptual vision is the source of the possible and timeless meaning they discern in the chaos around them. This timelessness appears in Pynchon's fiction in many guises (as the pervasive V.-mythology, as the "congruent" Tristero, as Mexico's statistical map and the Rilkean "angel's-eye view," and as the mandala integrations of the Rocket and the Zone-Hereros), but always it is the possibility that the Situation may be flush with meaning that drives the characters and permits them some relation to a world in which they are increasingly alienated.

A major source of that alienation is the fact of uncertainty and contingency in historical events which was discussed above. Because historical events result from a bewildering interplay of chance and intention, it is not possible to assign a cause to every effect; but, as in particle physics, such motion does admit of statistical analysis and may be explained in degrees of probability. This view of the historical process underlies Enzian's sense of the improbability of his own existence: "To those of us who survived von Trotha, it also means that we have learned to stand outside our history and watch it, without feeling too much. A little schizoid. A sense for the statistics of our being. One reason we grew so close to the Rocket, I think, was this sharp awareness of how contingent, like ourselves, the Aggregat 4 could be" (362).

Within Pynchon's books Enzian's schizoid understanding comes as close to the narrative intentions behind Pynchon's project as any single commentary affords. He holds within his conscious being, at once, the poles of free time and timeless determinism which puzzle and stifle the other characters. These poles are personified within Gravity's Rainbow by Edward Pointsman, champion of cause-and-effect history, and Roger Mexico, the modest statistician for whom historical events are not linked but may be plotted spatially by their distribution.

Mexico's statistical perspective is linked early in Gravity's Rainbow with Rilke's Angelic consciousness:[10] "Roger has tried to explain to [Jessica] the V-bomb statistics: the difference between distribution, in angel's-eye view, over the map of England, and their own chances, as seen from down here. She's almost got it: nearly understands his Poisson equation, yet can't quite put the two together" (54). The "angel's-eye view" has many expressions in Pynchon's writing, but it is the most exacting appropriation of a concept thus far by which Pynchon implies a meta-vision capable of binding the oppositions tearing his characters apart. Mexico's map is a spatial map of temporal events, and for the uninitiated seems to be a doorway into omniscience and safety. It is the very suggestiveness of the map which is important to Pynchon's project, for it represents the transformation of literal, consecutive experience into abstract, timeless meaning.

This abstraction of the literal is the technique by which Pynchon develops meaningfulness in his labyrinthine plots, and is analogous to Benny Profane's assimilation of street experience: "Profane had grown a little leery of streets, especially streets like this. They had in fact fused into a single abstracted Street, which come the full moon he would have nightmares about" (2). The literal "street," like Stencil's "literal pursuit" of V. (50), is eventually capitalized, which is the typographical transformation of meaningless detail into meaningful symbol. Profane's abstraction merges with Sidney Stencil's dual abstraction of the "hothouse" and the "street," and both concepts transcend the book's timebound plots to suggest a world of meaning competing with the piecemeal chaos within each episode. Pynchon's books are built on fugues of such words, escalating in vibrancy and overtones of meaning. His characters are caught in the dissonance between the literal and the abstract, for the transformations of their experience never advance them into absolute Meaning—what Oedipa calls "the direct, epileptic Word" (87).

Stencil Jr.'s "grand Gothic pile of inferences" becomes by the book's end a V-structure which overwhelms the historical details of the episodic plots. When Herbert arrives at last in Valletta, he feels V. everywhere in the city. His father, distributed elsewhere in Valletta's timelessness, experiences the same insight: "No time in Valletta. No history, all history at once" (456). Though the characters seek them out, these insights are unnerving; meaning is everywhere and engulfs plot. Events disconnected in time and space become exemplary of the same abstracted concept. Thus the technique of Pynchon's writing, the process of the words themselves, is a kind of consciousness identical with the consciousness of the characters those words describe. Stencil's accumulation of meanings around the letter "V" is also the book's design, and this identity accounts for the disconcerting reality Pynchon's books achieve. The engulfment of experience by its apparent meaning is both an analgesic for existential emptiness and a threat to Stencil's sense of personal freedom and the distinctness that girds his sanity.

Pynchon's fictions are built so that the reader is subjected to the same ambiguities which cripple the characters. The V-structure which threatens Herbert Stencil is larger than his particular plot line, and the uncertainties which surround V. and his relation to "her" become questions which the reader inherits in trying to determine V.'s relationship to events in the book. The event which closes V. is the apparently accidental death of Sidney Stencil. The prose describing the event reads flatly, like a set of directions (Pynchon was helping write "technical documents" at the Boeing Company for two years while working on V.):[11] "Draw a line from Malta to Lampedusa. Call it a radius." Impose an arbitrary order on this area of the Mediterranean, the words seem to say, but the waterspout which dashes Stencil's xebec occurs within the circle demarcated by the sailor Mehemet as the "domain" of Mara, goddess of Love and Maltese for "woman." Mehemet warns Stencil of her: "she will find ways to reach out from Valletta" (438). This is the last we hear of Mehemet and his timeless legend, but Pynchon intends us to recall the conversation and to be caught between two contradictory explanations of the same experience: either the waterspout is a freak accident, or Stencil's death is the result of another and simultaneous order of experience, in which the mechanical parody of the timeless goddess has reached out to destroy the "obsolete" diplomat, no longer useful in the century she presages.

A similar dissonance is established for the reader of *Gravity's Rainbow* in the image of the mandala. Circular, "fourfold expressions" (624) are distributed throughout the novel, and the narrator is visibly irked when Slothrop overlooks them. But these hints of integration are never made good on "this side" of the fiction, and this is the most provocative and important feature of Pynchon's writing, because it is the representation of the human experience of perceiving the world in parts while suspecting— and hoping—it is whole. Pynchon's characters do not experience the integration which exists except through the images they manufacture, including the integrations of the Rocket; this tease is advanced to the reader in the brilliant mapping of Tyrone's "girl-stars" onto Mexico's plotting of V-2 strikes: "But, well, it's a bit more than the distribution. The two patterns also happen to be identical. They match up square for square. The slides that Teddy Bloat's been taking of Slothrop's map have been projected onto Roger's, and the two images, girl-stars and rocket-strike circles, demonstrated to coincide" (85–86). Pointsman, naturally, thinks this is a reversal of cause and effect, which in a sense it is meant to be, though not as he construes it; the two together, stars within circles, form a mandala image permeating the book and represent the integration of love and death which the characters experience as opposing forces.

In this way meaning is an osmotic tissue between Pynchon's books and his readers, as they are enlisted in the same pattern-seeking which lures and afflicts the characters. Readers struggle to connect the fictional events of Pynchon's Situations with the more meaningful, narrative world implied by the patterns they discern. Like Jessica's effort to "put the two together," the struggle is never won because the dissonance is an inherent fact of the relationship between experience and meaning; characters and readers remain in the ambiguous middle ground of any informed relation to the Situation.

For Stencil, Oedipa, Leni Pokler, Tyrone, and others, the meaningful abstractions they seek to reify would be counterforces to the entropic tendencies of their cultural and material universes, but within the largest scope of Pynchon's fiction the continuity they seek includes those entropic tendencies, as well as the organizing efforts of the characters to retard them.

These organizing efforts are nothing less than acts of thought. Pynchon's writing puts tremendous obligations on thought and thinking, not to emphasize the possible solipsism of any perceived wholeness but to insist that the activity of thinking has an effect on the world analogous to the control of entropy through feedback.[12] This analogy is the basis of Wiener's cybernetic theory, and is used throughout Pynchon's writing as the fulcrum balancing the "enclaves of life" and the movement toward disorder. Thinking maintains an improbable order (often far from benign) in the face of that disorder. Drawing upon this source of metaphor, Pynchon puts the viability of renewal in thermodynamic terms: what are the chances for work?

The drama between the likelihood of decline and the chances for work is embodied in Herbert Stencil's motivations: "His random movements before the war had given way to a great single movement from inertness to—if not vitality, then at least activity. Work, the chase—for it was V. he hunted"—provide him with an "acquired sense of animateness" (44). This coupling of "inertness" with the animating power of search is the generative matrix for Pynchon's characters, and should be understood as the coupling of the inert with the active, of environment with character, of decay with structure. The ordering pursuits of Stencil and his progeny are part of a countervailing effort to think their worlds into wholeness by finding the key to social and personal history. Each narrative is a drama, in this sense, between the entropic tendencies of matter and the kinesis of thought.

The contours of this drama remain the same throughout Pynchon's fiction. Characters such as Stencil, Oedipa, and Tyrone move from a condition of lethargy in which "meaning" is not even an issue, to a pursuit of meaning which veers into paranoia, and whose virtue lies not so much in anything such seeking might accomplish as in the moral alertness it induces. These pursuits are their work, as Pynchon reminds us: Stencil's "chase" is his "work"; Oedipa's work in "sorting" Pierce's estate may "keep it all bouncing"; and Bodine tells Tyrone that what we need is "the physical grace to keep it working" (741).

Thought requires energy, but the meaning which thought discovers or brings into the world is a medium, not a message, and establishes a kinetic order as protective as it is inquisitive. Pynchon's books are neither Kabbalistic codes of salvation nor prophecies of doom; they do not ask us to choose among the extremes they document, but they do remind us of Sidney Stencil's "real present" and they make us see what McClintic Sphere finally saw: "that the only way clear of the cool/crazy flipflop was obviously slow, frustrating and hard work" (V., 342). The activity of thinking is hard work, and often discovers a reality which discourages thought; but man thinking is an "enclave of life" who keeps tension with the forces of decay. To keep this poise "between" is the most difficult of human tasks, but it is one in which we are aided by Pynchon's insistence on the importance of the ambiguous present.

NOTES

1. *The Human Use of Human Beings* (New York: Avon Books, 1967), p. 58.
2. *Kenyon Review*, 22 (1960), 277–92.
3. (New York: Ballantine Books, 1973), p. 1.
4. See *The Degradation of the Democratic Dogma* (New York: Macmillan, 1919).
5. "Lowlands" was published in *New World Writing*, no. 16 (1960), 85–108; "Under the Rose" appeared in *The Noble Savage*, no. 3 (1961), 223–51.
6. *Human Use*, pp. 13–15.
7. (Cambridge: Cambridge University Press, 1921), pp. 51, 56–7.
8. In the George Bull translation (Penguin, 1961), see pp. 130–33. Machiavelli's likening of Fortune to a "woman" is a simile Pynchon exploits in all his writing; in *Gravity's Rainbow* she becomes "Mistress of the Night." In this last book especially woman is the figure not only of the earth as Mother but of decay, putrescence, and death as well. Alvin Greenberg addresses this issue in his provocative article "The Underground Woman: An Excursion into the V-ness of Thomas Pynchon," *Chelsea*, no. 27 (1969), 58–65.

9. See Richard Schickel's "Paranoia at Full Cry," *World*, 2, no. 8 (Apr. 10, 1973), 43–44. Mr. Schickel disparages the "revue" as a "series of dreams, visions, or (more likely) dope-inspired hallucinations that bear little relationship to what has gone before or each other."

10. Rilke's idea of the "perfect consciousness" joining the visible and invisible, life and death, is important for an understanding of Pynchon's use of Rilke's poetry. The "Commentary" and appendices to the *Duino Elegies*, trans. J. B. Leishman and Stephen Spender (New York: Norton Library, 1963), are extremely helpful.

11. See Mathew Winston's interesting article "The Quest for Pynchon," in *Mindful Pleasures: Essays on Thomas Pynchon*, ed. George Levine and David Leverenz (Boston: Little, Brown, 1976), p. 260.

12. Wiener, *Human Use*, pp. 38–39 especially.

Two

The Crying of Lot 49:
"A Gentle Chill, an Ambiguity"

> "You were right to take this present
> interest in the dead."
> Oedipus Rex

Nowhere in recent fiction do we find a better example of finely wrought ambiguity than in Pynchon's second novel, *The Crying of Lot 49*. This book may be understood as the education of its central figure, Oedipa Maas, but it is an education which Pynchon complicates considerably by the uncertainty he introduces into every perception allowed to Oedipa and the reader. The major source of the ambiguity is Pynchon's figurative use of the concept of "entropy," for he exploits the diametrically opposite meanings which the term has in thermodynamics and in information theory.[1] Metaphorically, one compensates the other. In both, entropy is a measurement of disorganization, but in information theory disorganization increases the potential information which a message may convey, while in thermodynamics entropy is a measure of the disorganization of molecules within closed systems and possesses no positive connotation. Pynchon uses the concept of entropy in this latter sense as a figure of speech to describe the running down Oedipa discovers of the American Dream; at the same time he uses the entropy of information theory to suggest that Oedipa's sorting activities may counter the forces of disorganization and death.

Heat results from the motion of molecules. As Koteks explains to Oedipa, "Fast molecules have more energy than slow ones. Concentrate enough of them in one place and you have a region of high temperature. You can then use the difference in temperature between this hot region of the box and any cooler region, to drive a heat engine" (62). The "difference in temperature" is crucial, for without it there is no capacity for work. It is this difference which represents the organization of molecules. Entropy enters at this point: as the engine works, the two regions become mixed. The molecules collide with each other until they are all moving at the same rate, which means that eventually there is a cessation of difference, the creation of a static equilibrium, and an incapacity for work. Entropy is the measure of this declining activity, codified in the Second Law of Thermodynamics and summarized by Wiener in *The Human Use of Human Beings:* "energy spontaneously runs downhill in temperature."[2]

The apparent implication of this law is that everything is running down. Wiener formulates this in the most extreme terms: "As entropy increases, the universe, and all closed systems in the universe, tend naturally to deteriorate and lose their distinctiveness, to move from the least to the most probable state, from a state of organization and differentiation in which distinctions and forms exist, to a state of chaos and sameness."[3] This thesis was first put forward by Willard Gibbs, who used probability statistics to apply the Second Law to the universe at large. Henry Adams was quick to appropriate the thesis and apply it to his study of history in *The Degradation of the Democratic Dogma:* "to the vulgar and ignorant historian it meant only that the ash-heap was constantly increasing in size."[4]

Wiener also notes that "while the universe as a whole, if indeed there is a whole universe, tends to run down, there are local enclaves whose direction seems opposed to that of the universe at large and in which there is a limited and temporary tendency for organization to increase. Life finds its home in some of these enclaves."[5] He adds that there is disagreement among writers as to the possible application of the law of disorganization to biological and sociological systems. Following Adams, Pynchon borrows the concept and applies it to political and social situations in his short story "Entropy."

This story balances on the certainty of decline and the existence of "local enclaves" discussed by Wiener above, a balance which is visible in its binary composition. The activity of "Entropy" occurs within two distinct apartments, one above the other. In the lower apartment a character named Meatball is holding a lease-breaking party, while above him the character Callisto fears that a cold snap in Washington will not end.[6] Callisto's apartment is described in words which echo Wiener: "Hermetically sealed, it was a tiny enclave of regularity in the city's chaos, alien to the vagaries of the weather, of national politics, of any civil disorder" (279). The metaphoric connection between the heat-death of an isolated system and cultural decline is made by Callisto himself as he dictates his thoughts—Pynchon's parody of Adams's *Education*—to his companion Aubade:

"He was aware of the dangers of the reductive fallacy.... Nevertheless ... he found in entropy or the measure of disorganization for a closed system an adequate metaphor to apply to certain phenomena in his own world. He saw, for example, the younger generation responding to Madison Avenue with the same spleen his own had once reserved for Wall Street: and in American 'consumerism' discovered a similar tendency from the least to the most probable, from differentiation to sameness, from ordered individuality to a kind of chaos. He found himself, in short, restating Gibbs' prediction in social terms, and envisioned a heat-death for his culture in which ideas, like heat-energy, would no longer be transferred." (283–84)

Even though Callisto is aware of the fallacy of his own metaphor, he cannot escape it. Eventually, Aubade breaks a window, destroying the hermetic seal of their apartment; the two of them wait for the "moment of equilibrium ... when 37 degrees Fahrenheit should prevail both outside and inside, and forever, and the hovering, curious dominant of their separate lives should resolve into a tonic of darkness and the final absence of all motion" (292).

This suicide, however, is characteristic more of Callisto's response to the Second Law than of anything immediately apocalyptic about our culture. His neighbor, below, is faced with another social analogue of entropic disorganization, for Meatball's party is quickly disintegrating. But his response is the reverse of Callisto's:

Meatball stood and watched, scratching his stomach lazily. The way he figured, there were only about two ways he could cope: (a) lock himself in the closet and maybe eventually they would all go away, or (b) try to calm everybody down, one by one. (a) was certainly the more attractive alternative. . . . So he decided to try and keep his lease-breaking party from deteriorating into total chaos: he gave wine to the sailors and separated the *mura* players; he introduced the fat government girl to Sandor Rojas, who would keep her out of trouble; he helped the girl in the shower to dry off and get into bed; he had another talk with Saul; he called a repairman for the refrigerator which someone had discovered was on the blink. (291)

Callisto is abstract, a thinker; he sees into the thermodynamic future and despairs. He lives in ideas and absolute values; when those are not supported by the cultural and physical world around him, he gives up. Meatball, on the other hand, is one of the schlemihls of Pynchon's fiction who represent the obstinacy of plump vitality. Callisto's apocalyptic temperament prefers the "sense of an ending" to the difficulties of living in the middle.

Still, as intelligent readers, we know Callisto is correct, even while smiling at his premature resolution. The interplay between the two characters is exemplary of Pynchon's complexity: he dissociates thought from action, idea from feeling, allocating each to binary or opposing characters and plot lines. He pursues this technique in *V.* and makes it more convoluted in *The Crying of Lot 49*, which winds around a single character. His purpose is to frustrate the sentimental identification with either character or action; by doing so, he dramatizes within our response to his fiction—in our effort to join idea and feeling—the moral and psychic difficulty of living humanely with what we know to be true.

The binary dissociation of "Entropy" becomes the convoluted alienation of a single character in *The Crying of Lot 49*. Pynchon achieves this by writing in a conditional mode, so that the text itself oscillates like a standing wave between nodes of meaning, and by locating the paralyzing difficulties of those poles within the perceptions of Oedipa Maas. Her perceptions necessarily establish a middle ground between her culture and what she learns about it. Like the identity between Herbert Stencil's search for V. and the growth of the novel itself, Oedipa's instruction in American culture occurs under a McLuhanesque pedagogy that is also the method—almost the device—of *The Crying of Lot 49*.[7] Oedipa's task as executrix of Pierce Inverarity's estate forces her to examine her cultural medium whose message is alienation, loss, and death, "congruent with the cheered land" (135).

Oedipa is first "sensitized" to the technique of her education by the arrival of a letter from her husband Mucho, while she is staying in San Narciso: "It may have been an intuition that the letter would be newless inside that made Oedipa look more closely at its outside, when it arrived. At first she didn't see. It was an ordinary Muchoesque envelope, swiped from the station, ordinary airmail stamp, to the left of the cancellation a blurb put on by the government, REPORT ALL OBSCENE MAIL TO YOUR POTS-MASTER" (30). This is the beginning of her discovery of an alternative message service; once she acquires the McLuhanesque knack, she is quick to read the messages encoded in the medium of America, congruent with the ostensible signs it proffers.

By naming the town Pierce founded "San Narciso," Pynchon engages the reader in the habit of reading messages in the medium of the book at the same time we are pursuing Oedipa in her search. Pynchon's direct evocation of the Narcissus myth is a clear statement that Pierce's estate and what it represents are a culture in love with a dream-image of itself. In the myth Narcissus spurned the love of Echo, who was doomed to repeat only the last words of other voices. Pierce, like Narcissus, prefers the "deep vistas of space and time . . . allegorical faces that never were"—the colored windows of mute stamps—to Oedipa's spoken love. The Echo Courts where she stays become the scene of his first adultery, and—it is suggested—the beginning of her escape from the image of the tower which defines her at the end of chapter one (10–11). She will no longer be an Echo, but will try to say first things about real facts.

The origin of Pynchon's use of the Narcissus myth is Marshall McLuhan's *Understanding Media: The Extensions of Man*. The world of *The Crying of Lot 49* is built around those "extensions": word of mouth, letters and postal systems, telephones, television, information encoded in cars and mattresses, the written work in plays and bathrooms, even the configurations of cities and towns. In McLuhan's view all these are the narcissistic extensions of man whose medium is the message of his culture. McLuhan's interpretation of the Narcissus myth is readily available for

Pynchon's appropriation, for it establishes the identity between closed systems and narcissism:

Narcissus . . . is from the Greek word *narcosis,* or numbness. The youth Narcissus mistook his own reflection in the water for another person. This extension of himself by mirror numbed his perceptions until he became the servomechanism of his own extended or repeated image. The nymph Echo tried to win his love with fragments of his own speech, but in vain. He was numb. He had adapted to his extension of himself and had become a closed system.[8]

Pynchon incorporates this interpretation of the myth as social metaphor into *The Crying of Lot 49.* When Oedipa drives into San Narciso, she feels she is on the other side of the soundproof glass in a radio studio; the businesses are silent and paralyzed. The road along which San Narciso stretches Oedipa fancies is a "hypodermic needle, inserted somewhere ahead into the vein of a freeway, a vein nourishing the mainliner L.A., keeping it happy, coherent, protected from pain and whatever passes, with a city, for pain." In the Echo Courts themselves, "nothing moved" (13–15).

American culture, in short, is numb, and is addicted to what protects it from pain (and, ultimately, death). In McLuhan's terms our culture has become addicted to the material forms which the American Dream has assumed. Of course, the dream and the culture, like Narcissus and his image, are inseparable, and it is in this convolution that Oedipa finds herself. In the spray can caroming off the walls of the motel bathroom we have both an image of entropy—a region of fast molecules within the can exhausting itself within the confines of the bathroom—and an image of human life threatened, albeit comically, by the systems it has created. Oedipa "could imagine no end to it; yet presently the can did give up in midflight and fall to the floor" (23).

By the end of the book, Oedipa realizes that San Narciso is a microcosm of the Republic, an "incident among our climatic records of dreams and what dreams became among our accumulated daylight" (133). She understands that Pierce, the founder of this microcosm, had been seized by "some headlong expansion of himself" and remembers him telling her once: "Keep it bouncing, that's all the secret, keep it bouncing." This is her meditation amidst the transcontinental railroad tracks first laid by Pierce's hero, Jay Gould; the Second Law of Thermodynamics lurks in her language as Oedipa wonders that Pierce "must have known . . . how the bouncing would stop" (134).

Entropy and Information

The discussion thus far has concentrated on Pynchon's use of thermodynamic entropy; in this discussion *The Crying of Lot 49* is a view of America as a closed system running down. The bouncing will stop. But there is a convoluting wrinkle to all this, a hope of sorts which animates Oedipa's search for Tristero; this hope depends upon the concept of "information" and informational entropy. Both the Second Law and McLuhan's narcissism obtain within closed systems, for it is only within systems cut off from other sources of energy that the loss of the capacity for work is inevitable. Information, on the other hand, concerns what passes among systems. Wiener defines information as "the content of what is exchanged with the outer world as we adjust to it, and make our adjustment felt upon it."[9] Inverarity's advice—"Keep it bouncing"—is linked to the Second Law; "echoed" by Oedipa at the end of the book, this advice recalls Nefastis's dogmatism, which has its origin in information theory: "Communication is the key . . . to keep it all cycling" (77).

The Nefastis Machine represents a revision of Maxwell's hypothetical closed system with a sorting demon inside. Stanley Koteks's explanation of this to Oedipa (62) is correct, and so is her objection, "sorting isn't work?" Koteks's description and Oedipa's response are a fictionalized version of the distinction Wiener draws between contemporary physics and the physics of Clerk Maxwell's age:

In nineteenth century physics, it seemed to cost nothing to get information. The result is that there is nothing in Maxwell's physics to prevent one of his demons from furnishing its own power source. Modern physics, however, recognizes that the demon can only gain the information with which it [sorts the molecules] from something like a sense organ which for these purposes is an eye. The light that strikes the demon's eyes is not an energy-less component of mechanical motion, but shares in the main properties of mechanical motion itself. . . . In such a system, however, it will turn out that the constant collision between light and gas particles tends to bring the light and particles to an equilibrium. Thus while the demon may temporarily reverse the usual direction of entropy, ultimately it too will wear down.[10]

The temporary reversal is the result of "feedback." All our "modern automatic machines . . . possess sense organs; that is, receptors for messages coming from the outside."[11] Wiener stresses that in this capacity there is little difference between man and machine; both receive and transmit messages, and both survive in their environments through this feedback process, defined by Wiener as "the control of a machine on the basis of its *actual* performance rather than its *expected* performance." (The doors of an elevator are not only programmed to open at a designated floor, but the elevator also "knows" whether or not it is actually at that floor.) And it is this self-correcting ability of the machine which delays its running down.[12]

Oedipa's function, sitting beside the Nefastis Machine, is to "feed back something like the same quantity of information. To keep it all cycling" (77). The Machine, of course, is a comic distortion of the feedback systems Wiener is talking about. Nonetheless, it is a crucial interior metaphor of the book's operation as a whole. When Oedipa objects that "sorting is work," she ties the thermodynamic model to the book's postal courier themes, and to her own role as executrix. The first sentence of the book informs us that Pierce had "assets numerous and tangled enough to make the job of sorting it all out more than honorary" (1). Because Pierce's estate is a microcosm of America, the four parts to the metaphor are these: what Maxwell's Demon is to the Nefastis Machine, Oedipa is to America.

Pynchon's preoccupation with communications derives not only from McLuhan's "extensions of man" but from the central thesis of Wiener's book as well: "society can only be understood through a study of the messages and the communication facilities which belong to it; and that in the future development of these messages and communication facilities, messages between man and machines, between machines and man, and between machine and machine are destined to play an ever-increasing part."[13] Typically, this has a political importance for Pynchon. Emory Bortz imagines a member of Tristero in the seventeenth century declaring that "whoever could control the lines of communication, among all the princes, would control them" (123).

Oedipa's efforts to disentangle Inverarity's estate involve her in a study of her society; she comes to realize that her world is a vast communications system feeding her information which may engulf before it enlightens. Like the Demon, she tries to order the signs and symbols around her into some kind of operational meaning. But sorting is work, and she requires for this task some infusion of energy from the outside to counter the entropic movement inside toward disorganization, sameness, and death. Her role is bequeathed to her by Pierce, whose last name "Inverarity" is cognate with place names in Scotland where Clerk Maxwell—inventor of the Demon—was born. This is another of the messages coded in the text's medium, and it suggests that Pierce was the demon of his own system, which Oedipa, like all of us born into a system we did not create, bears the burden of keeping alive.

The Nefastis Machine not only connects the worlds of thermodynamics and information, but it casts a shadow on Oedipa's entire enterprise. Even Nefastis knows that his belief in his invention's workability rests on a visual metaphor: the identity of the equations for "entropy" in thermodynamics and the average unit in information theory.[14] The fact that they *look* the same but *mean* different things is a characteristic of clues in Pynchon's writing. This particular metaphor has added strength because in information theory "entropy" represents a measurement of possibility. J. R. Pierce (author of *Symbols, Signals and Noise: The Nature and Process of Communication*) tells us that "the amount of information conveyed by the message increases as the amount of uncertainty as to what message actually will be produced becomes greater. . . . The entropy of communication theory is a measure of this uncertainty."[15] Nefastis thinks the entropy of information theory is "positive" and can counter the "negative" entropy of thermodynamics. What makes the entropy metaphor "verbally graceful" and "objectively true" is his belief in the actual existence of Maxwell's Demon, sitting inside his machine. We must give Nefastis his due; he is as "bothered" by the word "entropy" as Oedipa is disturbed by "Trystero" (77), and the connection which he asserts is one with which theorists have been toying for as long as the similarity has been noticed.

Pierce discusses this matter in his chapter "Information Theory and Physics," and agrees with Wiener: "One pays a price for information which leads to a reduction of the statistical mechanical entropy of a system. This price is proportional to the communication-theory entropy of the message source which produces the information. It is always just high enough so that a perpetual motion machine of the second kind is impossible."[16] Such extratextual evidence undermines Nefastis's machine and implies that insofar as Oedipa is the sorting demon of her society, she is fighting a losing battle.

But in Oedipa, Pynchon has created a character with a knack for pointed questions. Her response to Koteks revealed the flaw in Maxwell's physics; her answer to Nefastis is equally incisive: "But what . . . if the Demon exists only because the two equations look alike? Because of the metaphor?" Nefastis merely smiles; he is a "believer" (78). The contrast between Oedipa's worried questioning and Nefastis's belief is a distinguishing characteristic of Oedipa's intelligence, but the distance she keeps from her own metaphors costs her dearly. They tease her with the possibility of meaning without providing the comfort Nefastis, and later her husband Mucho, enjoy.

On the freeway leading to San Francisco she compares her own search with the method of Nefastis, her thoughts interpolated through the narrative voice:

For John Nefastis (to take a recent example) two kinds of entropy, thermodynamic and informational, happened, say by coincidence, to look alike, when you wrote them down as equations. Yet he had made his mere coincidence respectable, with the help of Maxwell's Demon.

Now here was Oedipa, faced with a metaphor of God knew how many parts; more than two, anyway. With coincidences blossoming these days wherever she looked, she had nothing but a sound, a word, Trystero, to hold them together. (80)

That doubt is never expunged. At the end of the book the questions remain: is the Tristero pattern of Oedipa's own weaving, imposed on the world outside? Or is Tristero a pattern which inheres in the world outside, imposing itself upon her? Neither she nor the reader is allowed by Pynchon to ascertain the stable meaning of the blossoming pattern; without this certainty her usefulness in preserving order against a declining culture remains painfully ambiguous.

The early image of the tower (which closes chapter one) is a symbol of the uncertainty surrounding Oedipa's perceptions and our understanding of her condition. The tower quickly establishes an ambiguity which never resolves, for we are never sure whether it is an image of solipsism or one of imprisonment by forces outside Oedipa. Initially, the tower represents Oedipa's "buffered" and "insulated" existence at Kinneret-Among-the-Pines. Later, with Pierce in Mexico, the tower becomes an image of self-entrapment for her when she sees a painting by Remedios Varo titled "Bordando el Manto Terrestre," which pictures prisoners in a circular tower, "embroidering a kind of tapestry which spilled out the slit windows and into a void, seeking hopelessly to fill the void" (10).[17] By the end of the chapter the image has shifted again. Oedipa realizes that "her tower, its height and architecture, are like her ego only incidental: that what really keeps her where she is is magic, anonymous and malignant, visited on her from outside and for no reason at all" (11).

Oedipa does manage to escape the tower, but only increases her isolation.[18] She could join the anti-community available to her only by violating her integrity and accepting as literal truth the metaphorical linkages comprising Tristero (the replication of muted post horns, W.A.S.T.E. symbols, variations on the word "Tristero"). The people in the novel who do this—Nefastis, Mucho, Hilarius—are severely undercut by the narrator. They are facile believers in their own metaphors, while Oedipa rides a fence between a "hothouse" dogmatism on the one hand and engulfment by the void "outside" on the other. Indeed, *The Crying of Lot 49* may be read as a tragic account of the difficulty of human action in a world whose meanings are always *either* our own *or* just beyond our reach. Narcissism, in short, may be a condition of our participation in the world.

Information and Revelation

Pynchon plays on the religious implications of that ambiguity, for Oedipa's clues may be sacred signs as well as secular information, "*as if* . . . there were revelation in progress all around her" (italics mine, 28). Information is a species of "revelation" just as Nefastis's version of feedback is a species of California spiritualism. Both he and Wiener trade on the fact that information can provide a temporary and local reversal of entropy. To reiterate: "the Maxwell demon can work indefinitely . . . if additional light comes from outside the system and does not correspond in temperature to the mechanical temperatures of the particles themselves."[19] There are two requirements, then, for regenerating a system: the energy must come from an Outside, and it must be different from the energy present Inside. This is the importance of Tristero, for it represents the possible infusion from the outside of an organized "difference" reinstating opposition. The success of Oedipa's sorting rests directly on the uncertainty over the source of the information she accumulates and organizes into the Tristero; if these clues do not originate in a system or culture outside the one Oedipa seeks to redeem, then they are only a part of the inside system which is running down.

There are specific problems in her way. Pynchon's drama of contemporary society involves a historical as well as a spatial dimension. Oedipa's attempt to verify Tristero takes her into history, where she is confronted by various editions, pirated copies, questionable sources, and death. Oedipa can never get beyond herself, her language, or outside of time, but remains "parked at the centre of an odd, religious instant" (13). In some ways this book is about being trapped within the present, at an intersection of time and space. Talking with ninety-one-year-old Mr. Thoth— named for the Egyptian god of letters—she will feel "as if she had been trapped at the centre of some intricate crystal" (67). The story of Oedipa is the story of waiting for revelation, seeking it in the historical, secular, and time-bound world around her, but finding no God beyond the words she hopes will tell her the truth. Because she is trapped, "motion is relative"—which is the reason Pynchon includes the discussion at the Scope Bar about the Commodore Pinguid:

Off the coast of either what is now Carmel-by-the-sea, or what is now Pismo Beach, around noon or possibly toward dusk, the two ships sighted each other. One of them may have fired; if it did then the other responded; but both were out of range so neither showed a scar afterward to prove anything. Night fell. In the morning the Russian ship was gone. But motion is relative. If you believe an excerpt from the "Bogatir" or "Gaidamak"'s log, forwarded in April to the General-Adjutant in St. Petersburg and now somewhere in the Krasnyi Arkhiv, it was the "Disgruntled" that had vanished during the night. (32)

The Pinguid records are a comic parody of the unreliability (the relativity) of historical records, mimicked by the either/or prose of the narrator. The agility of metaphor balances on that ridge, as later, in a more somber scene, Oedipa realizes, "the act of metaphor . . . was a thrust at truth and a lie, depending where you were: inside, safe, or outside, lost" (95).

The sacred language which informs *The Crying of Lot 49* is a foil to the inverted, profane culture it describes: smog obscuring the feminine moon, waste, debris, the "empties" Bortz tosses at seagulls looking for the true sea, freeways built over graveyards, spray cans, rusting cars, shanties. All this is the iconography of isolation in a culture of throwaways. The ironic use of language has a fitting origin in Pierce's name, which derives from "petrus" or rock. As founder of San Narciso, Pierce is an inverse Peter, on whom is built the profane church of America. Pynchon enforces this irony immediately, for Oedipa—on reading that she has been named executrix—"stood in the living room, stared at by the greenish dead eye of the TV tube, spoke the name of God, tried to feel as drunk as possible" (1). Pierce occasions the association of the TV with God, and this association persists throughout the book, for the TV's "greenish eye" becomes the green bubble shades nearly everyone wears, which, like the TV, permit the wearer to be in someone else's living space without making contact.

Pynchon chooses Varo's painting, in part, because it serves for him as an inverse parable of creation. The world is created (in this painting) from the inside out; the rhythm of Pynchon's prose is an intentional echo of the opening verses of I John: "all the waves, ships and forests of the earth were contained in this tapestry, and the tapestry was the world" (10). Randy Driblette tells Oedipa, "That's what I'm for. To give the spirit flesh. The words, who cares? . . . I'm the projector at the planetarium, all the closed little universe visible in the circle of that stage is coming out of my mouth, eyes, sometimes other orifices also" (56). Driblette insists the play means nothing, yet Oedipa (and we) do not believe him fully because of his reluctance to speak about Tristero, and because of the accumulating coincidences. Varo's painting and Driblette threaten Oedipa with the possibility that there is no meaning beyond the one she herself weaves; but this possibility, while never denied, is never confirmed either.

Varo's painting is the initiation of a tapestry image which recurs three times late in the book. After interviewing Tremaine, Oedipa tells herself, "This is America, you live in it, you let it happen. Let it unfurl" (112). Here the painting, like the Narcissus myth, has been assumed into the fabric of the novel and is part of the social vision of a culture weaving itself in time, each generation responsible for the ongoing expansion. At the same time, there is no given pattern to follow. When she learns of Driblette's suicide, Oedipa mutters "subvocally—feeling like a fluttering curtain in a very high window, moving up to then out over the abyss" (114); she asks Bortz about Tristero "with the light, vertiginous sense of fluttering out over an abyss" (117). Earlier she worried that she was fashioning the tapestry, but now her paranoia has begun to blossom. She is not sure whether she is weaver or woven.

To resolve this uncertainty, Oedipa needs information not subject to time, "the direct, epileptic Word, the cry that might abolish the night" (87). This need underlies her desire to find out "something about the historical Wharfinger. Not so much the verbal one." Bortz tells her words are all we have. "Pick some words. . . . Them, we can talk about" (113). All that is available from the past is the medium in which Wharfinger lived, and the gambit of reaching the real message by tracing his words is blocked by the transformations of time: variant texts, pirated copies, faulty memory, and questionable interpretation. Her interest in Wharfinger, of course, arises from her determination to verify the literal existence of Tristero, because if Tristero is not part of some "grandiose practical joke" traceable to the Inverarity estate, then she may have found in it "a real alternative to the exitlessness, to the absence of surprise to life, that harrows the head of everybody American you know" (128).

Revelation and Tristero

When the Tristero alternative is examined, we find it linked with exile and death. Promises of "revelation" and "hierophany" are matched, symmetrically, by an opposing set of references to the "Book of the Dead" (18). The old man Oedipa interviews at Vesperhaven is Mr. Thoth, "scribe of the gods" in Budge's compilation of the *Egyptian Book of the Dead*.[20] Moreover, we read in C. G. Jung's "Psychological Commentary" to the *Tibetan Book of the Dead*: "Like *The Egyptian Book of the Dead*, it is meant to be a guide for the dead man during the period of his Bardo existence, symbolically described as an intermediate state of *forty-nine days'* duration between death and rebirth" (italics mine).[21] If the ending of *The Crying of Lot 49* is the point before revelation, then this revelation—at least in one sense—is death. Both Books of the Dead are about the necessary relation between the art of dying and the art of living. This relation is the fulcrum of one of Pynchon's fundamental themes: our culture is dying because it is predicated on a denial of death—as Tony Jaguar knew, for he had heard "stories about Forest Lawn and the American cult of the dead" (42).

The attributes of the Tristero alternative—exile, alienation, silence, waiting, disinheritance, darkness, and death—are all "congruent with the cheered land" (135). Oedipa's discovery of these attributes is concentrated in the "nighttown" section of the novel (chapter five), but this chapter has been prefigured twice by prose that anticipates her passage through the night and establishes resonances which convolute what she learns there. The passage-through-the-night theme is initiated in her motel room with Metzger. As the Strip Botticelli game unwinds toward climax, Oedipa suspects "that if the sun ever came up Metzger would disappear. She wasn't sure if she wanted him to" (26). Despite the humor of this scene, the chapter can be read (as the narrator points out in chapter three) as the beginning of Oedipa's escape from the tower. That means an increase in "intensity," "focus," and a removal of the "insulation" she experienced at Kinneret. With Metzger she strips herself naked, and this venturesome adultery is only the first of many examples in the novel in which her efforts to "communicate" result in increased isolation (see 114).

Her night with Metzger is recalled and expanded by a passage ten pages later:

So began, for Oedipa, the languid, sinister blooming of The Tristero. Or rather, her attendance at some unique performance prolonged as if it were the last of the night, something a little extra for whoever'd stayed this late. As if the break-away gown, net bras, jeweled garters and G-strings of historical figuration that would fall away were layered dense as Oedipa's own streetclothes in that game with Metzger in front of the Baby Igor movie; as if a plunge toward dawn indefinite black hours long would indeed be necessary before The Tristero could be revealed in its terrible nakedness. Would its smile, then, be coy, and would it flirt away harmlessly backstage, say good night with a Bourbon Street bow and leave her in peace? Or would it instead, the dance ended, come back down the runway, its luminous stare locked to Oedipa's, smile gone malign and pitiless; bend to her alone among the desolate rows of seats and begin to speak words she never wanted to hear? (36)

The structure of the passage is the same as that in chapter two: passage through the night, the stripping away of clothes/figurations, and the promise of revelation toward dawn. This simile complicates the relationship of Oedipa to the Tristero, for the historical strip tease is likened to Oedipa's own in the previous chapter, and this prompts the inescapable suspicion that Oedipa and Tristero are somehow involved in one another, and that Oedipa herself—as her name suggests—may be at the heart of the declining society. With this finesse, Pynchon convolutes outside and inside; the comfortable distinction between Oedipa and Tristero is now complicated. At her hotel in Berkeley Oedipa "kept waking from a nightmare about something in the mirror. . . . When she woke in the morning, she was sitting bolt upright, staring into the mirror at her own exhausted face" (74). Back in southern California she dreams "of disembodied voices from whose malignance there was no appeal, the soft dusk of mirrors out of which something was about to walk . . ." (131).

The two passages just discussed prefigure Oedipa's descent into the San Francisco night and become the structure of that chapter. The preparation for our view of her experience is echoed in the language: "At some indefinite passage in night's sonorous score, it also came to her that she would be safe, that something, perhaps only her linearly fading drunkenness, would protect her. The city was hers, as, made up and sleeked so with the customary words and images (cosmopolitan, culture, cable cars) it had not been before: she had safe-passage tonight to its far blood's branchings" (86–87). During the night the metaphors (like "historical figurations") will fall away. The city, "made up and sleeked," does a strip tease, which is an externalized version of the clichés that are falling away from Oedipa's understanding. The children she meets are unafraid because "they had inside their circle an imaginary fire, and needed nothing but their own unpenetrated sense of community" (87), but Oedipa's own protection begins to dissolve because she is not a believer and because her world has been pierced. The only community she discovers is an anti-community, like the Inamorati Anonymous who have nothing to share but a mutual isolation from one another, "dedicated not to continuity but to some kind of interregnum" (91).

Oedipa's passage through the night is fulfilled at dawn when she comes upon the drunken sailor and confronts for the first time the "irreversible process" of death. This is the revelation which greets her at dawn, and accompanying it is a realization which helps explain the book's slippery ambiguity. Oedipa's thoughts pun on the DTs she feels in the sailor's body, and she remembers that in calculus "dt" meant "also a time differential, a vanishingly small instant in which change had to be confronted at last for what it was, where it could no longer disguise itself as something innocuous like an average rate; where velocity dwelled in the projectile though the projectile be frozen in mid-flight, where death dwelled in the cell though the cell be looked in on at its most quick" (95–96). The "delta-t" is a mathematical expedient for assuming continuous motion where none can be shown, and the shorthand "dt" establishes the continuity in Oedipa's understanding between the sailor's delirium tremens and the irreversible process.

Oedipa realizes suddenly that language is a kind of linguistic membrane between literal experience and what that experience may mean:

The saint whose water can light lamps, the clairvoyant whose lapse in recall is the breath of God, the true paranoid for whom all is organized in spheres joyful or threatening about the central pulse of himself, the dreamer whose puns probe ancient fetid shafts and tunnels of truth all act in the same special relevance to the word, or whatever it is the word is there, buffering, to protect us from. The act of metaphor then was a thrust at truth and a lie, depending where you were: inside, safe, or outside, lost. Oedipa did not know where she was. (95)

From the outside, metaphor is only a "buffer," while from the "inside, safe," metaphor provides access to that very realization, and is therefore a "thrust at the truth." The text of *The Crying of Lot 49* is fully metaphoric in that sense, existing in the middle between inside and outside, between a reductive literalism in which words are mere tools standing for things, and a speculative symbolism in which words are signs capable of pointing toward realities which transcend those signs. This is the same linguistic space as that occupied by Oedipa and the reader. If we look again at the formulation in the book, we see that metaphor is both a "thrust at truth and a lie"; it becomes disjunctive, or relative, only as it is employed from one side or the other. With this in mind, the next sentence is crucial: "Oedipa did not know where she was." At the end of the book she is still between "the zeroes and ones." Like Oedipa, the reader too is left in the middle, because *The Crying of Lot 49* stubbornly refuses to allow its own linguistic symmetries to resolve in ways that Oedipa's do not.

When Oedipa returns to visit Mike Fallopian at the Scope, he proposes that the entire Tristero network is a hoax. Her reaction is conveyed in a telling simile: "like the thought that someday she would have to die, Oedipa had been steadfastly refusing to look at the possibility directly" (126). If the hoax is real, then death is "only death" (137). The Tristero alternative is a release from her "deckful of days," but it is a release into a reality that recognizes death. Oedipa's search thus involves an unwitting discovery of her own mortality, a fact deadened by her daytime suburban culture but "congruent" with it.

As the world about her takes on more and more the character of information, Oedipa's evidence seems less like truth than clue to something beyond it; this is because her medium and its message are identical. Oedipa is caught in the midst of this identity. Her medium—housing tracts, the media, people, roads, graveyards, Cohen's dandelion wine—is all message; messages, she realizes, are subject to time and decay. Oedipa knows the sailor will die and with him all the messages encoded in his life. In her private vision of conflagration, she prophesies that his mattress will burn:

She remembered John Nefastis, talking about his Machine, and massive destructions of information. So when this mattress flared up around the sailor, in his Viking's funeral: the stored, coded years of uselessness, early death, self-harrowing, the sure decay of hope, the set of all men who had slept on it, whatever their lives had been, would truly cease to be, forever, when the mattress burned. She stared at it in wonder. It was as if she had just discovered the irreversible process. (95)

Her memory of Nefastis reminds us that the price of work done is entropy. This image of the burning sailor is the fulfillment of Oedipa's earlier suspicion that she might be "left with only compiled memories of clues, announcements, intimations, but never the central truth itself, which must somehow each time be too bright for memory to hold; which must always blaze out, destroying its own message irreversibly" (69).

As message, life's medium is the transmutation of waste. Like the lost Faggio Guard, all life is transformed into the medium of the present. This process is described by Wiener in his chapter "Organization as the Message." Organisms are viewed by him as messages, since they are "opposed to chaos, to disintegration, to death, as message is to noise." Organisms, Wiener points out, exist not as substantial entities but as patterns whose content is fluid. The pattern resists disorganization, not the substance: "We are but whirlpools in a river of ever-flowing water. We are not stuff that abides, but patterns that perpetuate themselves."[22] On this point, Wiener and McLuhan dovetail for Pynchon; Oedipa comes to view the universe as a message. As her talent for sensing meaning behind pattern ripens, the patterns proliferate and haunt her, "as if (as she'd guessed that first minute in San Narciso) there were revelation in progress all around her" (28).

Oedipa's revelation, such as it is, is secular and real, and is the realization of loss and death. *The Crying of Lot 49* is a book about loss, about the tragedy of what happens to the moment in the stream of time. The truth existing in the present recedes into the past and is never present to our knowledge. Still, she is surrounded by transmutations of the past: she drinks it in Cohen's dandelion wine, just as the evil Duke writes with the ink of the Lost Guard. Mucho understood this when he worked as a used car salesman, watching people bring in "motorized, metal extensions of themselves" full of the "actual residue" of their lives "like a salad of despair" (4–5). Pynchon has created in the W.A.S.T.E. postal system an inverse acronym, for We Await Silent Tristero's Empire stands for "waste." Waste is a communications system; as the medium of our society, its message is plain.

Oedipa is educated to this message, and learns about the subterranean congruence of poverty and disease which lies beneath the shine of America's countenance. Therefore she is not a static character but one who changes and moves toward something new (12). Near the end of the book she experiences a secular epiphany:

She stood between the public booth and the rented car, in the night, her isolation complete, and tried to face toward the sea. But she'd lost her bearings. . . . San Narciso at that moment lost (the loss pure, instant, spherical, the sound of a stainless orchestral chime held among the stars and struck lightly), gave up its residue of uniqueness for her; became a name again, was assumed back into the American continuity of crust and mantle. (133)

This instant parallels the insight occasioned by Varo's painting that the land she stood on "was only by accident known as Mexico" (11). Oedipa now understands that her ego, like Narciso, is only "incidental"—"a name; an incident among our climatic records of dreams and what dreams became among our accumulated daylight. . . . There was the true continuity" (133–34). Paradoxically, the word "continuity" has come to mean in the course of the novel its exact opposite. For all Oedipa's admirable courage and persistence, she still possesses—like Herbert Stencil in pursuit of V.—a naive hope that Tristero will be a tangible and literal person (137). Yet it is clear that Tristero's reality is metaphoric; while it is an alternative, it is one indissolubly knit to the culture that alienates it. The pattern Oedipa finds or weaves has the reality of all metaphors, just as the community she discovers is real, though the word "community" here is a metaphor for the lack of community we all share.

At the beginning of The Crying of Lot 49 the reader encourages

Oedipa in her escape from the tower; by the end of the book she is outside lost, and paralyzed by the "matrices of a great digital computer." This is Pynchon's image of a culture whose terms— as Sidney Stencil predicted—have been reduced to polar extremes. Oedipa is caught between the suburban culture she has outgrown and the communion of withdrawal. She is happy with neither option; Oedipa "had heard all about excluded middles; they were bad shit, to be avoided; and how had it ever happened here, with the chances once so good for diversity?" If there is no Tristero "beyond the appearance of the legacy of America," then there is "just America" and the "only way she could continue, and manage to be at all relevant to it, was as an alien, unfurrowed, assumed full circle into some paranoia" (136–37). The image of the computer, while inherently apt, may have its ironic source in the optimism of *Understanding Media:* "The computer . . . promises by technology a Pentecostal condition of universal understanding and unity."[23] By contrast, Pynchon demonstrates the "secular miracle of communication": tremendous connectedness, but no community.

If hope exists at all, it is in the ability to withstand the terrible ambiguity threatening Oedipa. The fictions Pynchon writes have no happy endings; they hardly seem to "end" at all, for there is no end to the ambiguities his writing provokes. Oedipa does achieve an awareness of her culture, and that awareness is never held in doubt. Yet the doubts which her culture propagates are never resolved. To her credit she maintains her ground instead of slipping into a hermetic dogmatism or an apocalyptic suicide. Her position is isolated and filled with a paranoia more protective than psychotic. Yet with Oedipa we experience a broadening of consciousness, and a sense of the possibility for meanings which inhere in the world and in language. Those meanings, most skillfully in *The Crying of Lot 49,* depend for their vitality on the suspension in which they are caught. And this is one of the extra-literary aspects of the book, for insofar as *The Crying of Lot 49* stakes out the necessary ambiguity in which moral actions must take place, the narrator's binary flip-flopping not only makes our reading experience commensurate with Oedipa's trials, but echoes the experience beyond our reading.

NOTES

1. This use of the various senses of "entropy" has been widely discussed but with varying conclusions. See Joseph Slade, *Thomas Pynchon* (New York: Warner Paperback Library, 1974); Edward Mendelson's "The Sacred, the Profane and *The Crying of Lot 49*," in *Pynchon: A Collection of Critical Essays*, ed. Edward Mendelson (Englewood Cliffs, N.J.: Prentice-Hall, 1978), pp. 112–46; and Anne Mangel, "Maxwell's Demon, Entropy, Information: *The Crying of Lot 49*," in *Mindful Pleasures*, ed. Levine and Leverenz, pp. 87–100.

2. *Human Use*, p. 42.

3. *Ibid.*, p. 20.

4. *Degradation*, p. 142.

5. *Human Use*, pp. 20–21.

6. See Robert Redfield and Peter L. Hays, "Fugue as Structure in Pynchon's 'Entropy,'" *Pacific Coast Philology*, 12 (1977), 50–55.

7. In a letter from Thomas Pynchon to Thomas F. Hirsch, Pynchon refers to McLuhan several times. See Joseph Slade's "Escaping Rationalization: Options for the Self in *Gravity's Rainbow*," *Critique*, 18, no. 3 (1977), n. 2.

8. *Understanding Media: The Extensions of Man*, 2d ed. (New York: New American Library, 1964), p. 51.

9. *Human Use*, pp. 26–27.

10. *Ibid.*, pp. 43–44.

11. *Ibid.*, p. 33.

12. *Ibid.*, pp. 35–36.

13. *Ibid.*, p. 25.

14. For a pictorial view of this identity, see Mangel, "Maxwell's Demon."

15. (New York: Harper & Row, 1961), p. 23.

16. *Ibid.*, p. 206.

17. See David Cowart's "Pynchon's *The Crying of Lot 49* and the Paintings of Remedios Varo," *Critique*, 18, no. 3 (1977), 19–26.

18. My thinking here was influenced by Edward Mendelson's fine piece on this book (see above, note 1). In his view *The Crying of Lot 49* is a good deal more invigorating than I take it to be. Mendelson is more satisfied with the metaphoric way of comprehending the world than Oedipa is; she wants the metaphor incarnate.

19. *Human Use*, p. 44.

20. Sir E. A. Budge, 3 vols. in 1 (New York: Barnes & Noble, 1969), p. 25.

21. Comp. and ed. W. Y. Evans-Wentz (New York: Oxford University Paperback, 1960), p. xxxv.

22. *Human Use*, p. 130.

23. McLuhan, *Understanding Media*, p. 84.

Three

Pynchon's Great Song

"There's no calling it back. Either
he lets the harp go, his silver chances
of song, or he has to follow."

"Over the Rainbow"

The world has become increasingly available to us as image; with
the advent of film this second-order reality has reached the per-
fection of a false continuity: false images which move. Book 3 of
Gravity's Rainbow, the picaresque "In the Zone," begins with
this epigraph: "Toto, I have a feeling we're not in Kansas any
more. . . ." *The Wizard of Oz*, starring Judy Garland, was released
in 1939 (when Thomas Pynchon was two years old). The thirties
was an era of the child-star: the Gum sisters, Shirley Temple, and
Mickey Rooney (to mention those Pynchon includes). In the
midst of the depression, can an entire civilization, seeing itself
decay, believe in the redeeming power of The Child? And can we,
"old fans who've always been at the movies," (760) see beyond the
celluloid we paid for to the life it protects us from? Slothrop,
calming his fears by the homeopathy of investigating V-2 bomb
sites, finds "alive, a little girl, half-suffocated under a Morrison
shelter. Waiting for the stretcher, Slothrop held her small hand,
gone purple with the cold." To her first words, "Any gum,
chum?"

all he had for her was a Thayer's Slippery Elm. He felt like an idiot. Before
they took her off she brought his hand over to kiss anyway, her mouth
and cheek in the flare lamps cold as frost, the city around them at once a
big desolate icebox, stale-smelling and no surprises inside ever again. At
which point she smiled, very faintly, and he knew that's what he'd been
waiting for, wow, a Shirley Temple smile, as if this exactly canceled all
they'd found her down in the middle of. What a damn fool thing. (24–25)

So it isn't even real children who redeem, but the continuity of their images on reels of film.

The writer Gerfaut, in *V.*, speculates that "the young girl—adolescent or younger—had again become the mode in erotic fiction" (377). The chapter "V. in love" paints the yellow, rainless decadence of pre–World War I Europe (echoes of Wilde, parodies of Eliot). V. loves Melanie, a fifteen-year-old ballerina who is for her a "fetish,"—"not real but an object of pleasure." In *The Crying of Lot 49* Oedipa's "one extra-marital fella" elopes "with a depraved 15-year-old" (114).

The inanimate image is more erotic than the reality itself, and the undeveloped girl becomes an object in the hands of an old civilization, projecting its dreams upon her. So in *Gravity's Rainbow* Franz Pokler, aroused by Margherita Erdmann in the pornographic *Alpdrücken*, returns home not to sleep with his wife Leni but to act out the film he has just seen, "fucking her into some submission. . . . How many other men, shuffling out again into depression Berlin, carried the same image back from *Alpdrücken* to some drab fat excuse for a bride?" (397). Ilse is the film-child issue of that night, and Bianca—fathered on Margherita during a gang rape at the movie's filming—is her "shadow" double on the other side of the silver screen. Later, aboard the ship *Anubis*, Bianca does a "perfect mimickry" of Shirley Temple singing "On the Good Ship Lollipop." For refusing an encore, Greta beats her with a steel ruler while the passengers—aroused by this treatment of Bianca as an object—engage in an orgy whose convolutions are a model of decadence. Afterward Bianca seduces Slothrop, but Tyrone leaves her because he prefers the erotic image to the real thing ("No difference between a boxtop and its image, all right, their whole economy's based on *that* . . . ," 472). Pointsman haunts the waiting rooms of bus stations, lusting after the tattered children (50–51). Slothrop himself was sold "like a side of beef" as an object of Jamf's experiments, and Blicero sent Gottfried aloft inside the premier machine of our age. Age corrupts the youth it brings into the world, and this is but one pervasive example of Pynchon's criticism of a civilization that manufactures a plastic continuity to laminate its own fragmented reality.

Oppressed by her own set of adults, Dorothy sang this song (they gave it an Academy Award for "Best Song"):

Some-day I'll wish up-on a star and
wake up where the clouds are far be-hind me,
Where troubles melt like lem-on drops,
a-way a-bove the chim-ney tops that's where you'll find me.
Some-where O-ver The Rain-bow blue-birds fly,
Birds fly O-ver The Rain-bow, why then oh why can't I?
If hap-py lit-tle blue-birds fly be-yond the rainbow,
why oh why can't I?[1]

It seemed to answer a need. Next year's "Best Song" went to "When You Wish upon a Star" (sung by Jiminy Cricket in the cartoon film *Pinocchio*, 1940).

As part of the oblique irony present in Pynchon's use of *The Wizard of Oz*, *Gravity's Rainbow* is provided with the trappings of a film version of a 1940s musical, complete with "acid" colors (448), a clarinet "out at sea" (225), and updated lyrics to tunes like "Pretty Baby" ("Ev'ry little Nazi's shootin' pool or playin' potsy") and "Bye-Bye Blackbird" ("Got a hardon in my fist, / Don't be pissed, / Re-enlist— / Snap—to, Slothrop!"). The appearance of these and other suggestions of theatre above the text corresponds to the characters' paranoid suspicions that they are only actors in a drama being directed by someone else; the medium of the text underlines the book's opening conviction that "it's all theatre."

Film and our relation to it are for Pynchon an allegory of free will and determinism, and participate in the paradoxes of relativity discussed in Chapter One. The outlines of this allegory are explicit in the wager between Metzger and Oedipa over the outcome of the film *Cashiered*, in which Metzger played Baby Igor. The entire footage of the film—its "time" or history—is present to Metzger; for Oedipa, the film's unwinding is like mortal time, its end unpredictable. Oedipa's bet is made freely, though the end (of the movie) is predetermined. Sitting in its circular can, the reel is timeless, "light can't fatigue it, it can be repeated endlessly" (20); like a four-dimensional continuum, episodes recorded in time exist on film in space. As such, film is a model of continuity we can project but not experience, though we may suspect "it's all theatre."

Film is allied therefore with other types of spurious continuity in Pynchon's writing, and is exemplary of an analytic consciousness in the West (fittingly typified in *Gravity's Rainbow* as "the German mind") that separates life's motion into still frames, which are then pieced together "to counterfeit movement" (407). Paradoxically, this technique has arisen from a compulsion to understand or find the continuity of motion, which Zeno has shown to be incomprehensible. Zeno's paradox was finessed, mathematically, by Leibniz's invention of calculus; the two concepts, film and calculus, are integrated in *Gravity's Rainbow* in the engineers' films of the Rocket: "There has been this strange connection between the German mind and the rapid flashing of successive stills to counterfeit movement, for at least two centuries—since Leibniz, in the process of inventing calculus, used the same approach to break up the trajectories of cannonballs through the air" (407).

These methods are generalized in Pynchon's writing as techniques of mass manipulation which is self-producing, leaching through the culture. Pynchon's ability to convey such leaching is one of his extraordinary powers, first apparent in the nightmarish (and false) nostalgia imposed on the members of his party by Foppl, "the siege party's demon, who was in fact coming more and more to define his guests assembled, to prescribe their common dream" (*V.*, 237). Through his "habits of observation" Mondaugen was able to escape the dream, but he watches Godolphin succumb to the memory of 1904. The old man is last seen in drag, flicking the buttocks of a Bondel, enjoying a decadent memory of something he never experienced (259). In the lexicon of *Gravity's Rainbow* Godolphin was "put on the Dream" (697). In a more benign area of *V.* the dentist Eigenvalue theorizes that it is just our compartmentalization within cycles of time which produces this warped relation to the past, so that "we are charmed by the funny-looking automobiles of the '30's, the curious fashions of the '20's, the peculiar moral habits of our grandparents. We produce and attend musical comedies about them and are conned into a false memory, a phony nostalgia about what they were. We are accordingly lost to any sense of a continuous tradition" (141). The film musical of *Gravity's Rainbow* upends any sentimentalism (in this parody of "Queen for a Day"): "'—yes, you, Marine Captain Esberg from Pasadena—*you*, have just had, the Mystery Insight! (gasps and a burst of premonitory applause) and so *you*—are our *Paranoid . . . For The Day!* . . . Yes, it *is* a movie! Another World War II situation comedy, and your chance to find out what it's *really like*'" (691–92).

Earlier in *Gravity's Rainbow*, in the moving Pokler section, Franz is unsure whether the successive girls who appear in his barrack each summer are his daughter or a "movie." The narrator tells us that Pokler "was about to be given proof that these techniques had been extended past images on film, to human lives" (407), but Pokler's uncertainty over the girl's identity is left unresolved as a demonstration that continuity for mortals (here, now) is a matter of choice: "Pokler knew that while he played, this would have to be Ilse—truly his child, truly as he could make her. It was the real moment of conception, in which, years too late, he became her father" (421).

This continuity is of a radically different type from his dreams as a member of the amateur rocketeers in the Verein für Raumschiffahrt. Those dreams found expression in a film which Pynchon has Pokler and Leni view, Fritz Lang's *Die Frau im Mond* (1928). Hermann Oberth, author of *Die Rakete zu den Planetenräumen* ("The Rocket into Interplanetary Space") and member of the VfR, was technical advisor for Lang. Pynchon's account comes from Walter Dornberger's *V-2* and Willy Ley's *Rockets, Missiles and Space Travel*.[2] The VfR engineers are faced with starvation: "The choice was between building what the Army wanted—practical hardware—or pushing on in chronic poverty, dreaming of expeditions to Venus" (*GR*, 400–401). The VfR submits to the Army's bureaucracy; Pokler's wife Leni objects: "'They're using you to kill people,' Leni told him, as clearly as she could. 'That's their only job, and you're helping them.' 'We'll all use *it*, someday, to leave the earth. To transcend.'" Like Dorothy, Franz wants to fly over the rainbow.

The rainbow has been a sign studied by men for thousands of years. In African mythologies it is commonly a devouring serpent come out to graze after the rain; the Greeks called it Iris, messenger of the gods; to the Hebrews it was a sign of God's covenant with man. (An interesting treatment is Carl Boyer's *The Rainbow: From Myth to Mathematics*.[3]) The attempt to explain the multi-colored parabola in the sky led Newton to his discoveries with the prism. His theory of light developed from his study of the rainbow, and persistent efforts to understand light in all its manifestations took us to the realization that matter equals energy.

Before the twentieth century the nature of color had been understood well enough to reveal that what we see is but a reflection of wavelengths not absorbed, a breaking up of pure, colorless light into its component spectra; this revelation yielded these dour thoughts from Melville's "The Whiteness of the Whale": ". . . and when we proceed further, and consider that the mystical cosmetic which produces every one of her hues, the great principle of light, for ever remains white or colorless in itself, and if operating without medium upon matter, would touch all objects, even tulips and roses, with its own blank tinge—pondering all this, the palsied universe lies before us a leper." Sixty years after *Moby-Dick* this passage becomes a workable definition of the way films project: light, operating through a medium, upon matter. *Gravity's Rainbow* is a book about light and reminds us that our relation to light in space is also our location in time. In a universe where matter and energy are interchangeable, where quite literally we may say that everything is Light, our place within it permits us only a narrow band of color playing across the silver screen of the human theatre.

Film counterfeits this fact, and conspires in the thorough enterprise of manipulation which the book's paranoid vision suggests. Imipolex G, we are told, "has proved to be nothing more—or less—sinister than a new plastic, an aromatic heterocyclic polymer" (249), a creation of plasticity's ability to counterfeit nature. By the end of *Gravity's Rainbow* Imipolex G has become the elusive symbol of The Man's presence embedded in (what used to be) our most private instincts, susceptible to stimulation by "the projection, *onto* the Surface, of an electronic 'image,' analogous to a motion picture" (700). These are movies within movies. "It's all theatre," the first page tells us; later, the non-serial scenes which replace the cause-and-effect narrative are a "nonstop revue" crossing the stage of the "Schein-Aula" or "Seeming-Hall" (681/687).

When Dorothy, Toto, & Co. cross into Oz, the film—formerly in black and white—bursts into color. Following the yellow-brick road, they find a wizard who is nothing but a fraud but whose defensive, good-hearted wisdom provides all the characters with certification of the qualities they already possess. Color is associated with the land beyond the rainbow, with make-believe, weird characters, and witches. Oz is also the allegorical land of dreams in which Dorothy tries to resolve her differences with the black and white world of Kansas. The film gives Dorothy her wish; she and Toto return home. But Tyrone never escapes the Zone. After following Albert Krypton's directions up the "yellow-brick road," Slothrop arrives at Putzi's, a landed version of the *Anubis's* decadence, where he narrowly escapes castration, and leaves without the faked Army discharge he needs for return to America. That comparison alone reveals something about the book, as does the title: this rainbow is not God's (Who?). If there's any covenant to be made, it's with Gravity (What?). What we seek lies under, not over (here:now).

Jung and Extensions beyond the Self

All of Pynchon's fiction may be said to teeter on the fulcrum between a continuity which is real but inaccessible, and continuities which are accessible but false. To read *Gravity's Rainbow* with any kind of comfort, we must recognize the book as making available to us continuities beyond the "primacy of the 'conscious' self and its memories" (*GR*, 153). This is both theme and method. As theme, the "primacy of the 'conscious' self" organizes this nexus of ideas:

- waking consciousness
- rationality
- linear memory as base of coherent self
- the "one-way flow of European time" (724)
- the scientific tradition of Analysis
- the cause and effect mechanistic world view

u.s.w.

As narrative method, extensions beyond the self permit Pynchon to write outside the one-way time his characters inhabit. Opposed to the "self" as consciousness and memory is a sense of the "self" as *intersection*. Weber calls it *Sinnzusammenhang* (his translators write "complex of meaning"),[4] and Rilke the "senses' crossroad."[5] It is a lesson the twentieth century has been learning since Planck first established quantum physics in 1900: not an electron, but patterns of energy. In 1927 Heisenberg showed us we cannot determine simultaneously both the position and velocity of a subatomic particle. Physics has become statistical, and the mechanical dream of showing how each particle caused this or that measurable effect had to be discarded. Hence Mexico to Pointsman: "'I wonder if you people aren't a bit too—well, strong, on the virtues of analysis. I mean, once you've taken it all apart, fine, I'll be the first to applaud your industry. But other than a lot of bits and pieces lying about, what have *you* said?'" And Pointsman's response: "'Pavlov believed that the ideal, the end we all struggle toward in science, is the true mechanical explanation. . . . No effect without cause, and a clear train of linkages'" (88–89). Pointsman in 1945 is an anachronism, though not without power. In the face of the uncertainty both Heisenberg and Gödel establish in the relation between perception and the world perceived, and out of fear of the world of chance personified in the random falling of V-2 rockets, Pointsman seeks control of the man who embodies these heresies, Tyrone Slothrop.

By contrast, the narrator of *Gravity's Rainbow* asks us to believe in spirits of transformation given voice: Roland Feldspath on the "other side" of death; Lyle Bland taken away magically; Pirate Prentice "haunted"—able to live the dreams of others, freeing them psychically for their work. Later, the experience which forces Pirate to confront his own freedom and guilt is a dream of his own (537–48); the knowledge he gains "there" (among other double agents who have ceased yearning for innocence and some ground on which they are guiltless) will be put to use in his dialogue with the newly enlightened Mexico. The dreams and spiritualist visitations of the characters Feldspath, Rathenau, Blobadjian, and Bland are part of Pynchon's design to create a ubiquitous present which undermines the rationalist enterprises of Pointsman and the men above him. The imagery of their determinist schemes in *Gravity's Rainbow*—ice, whiteness, snow, gray skies, and pearl-colored London fog—is embodied in Pointsman (whose place of work is "The White Visitation") and his trained gray octopus Grigori, sent to the Riviera to do battle with the gaudy Tyrone in his Hawaiian shirt.

The spirits share a common theme, first enunciated by Feldspath: "The illusion of control. That A could do B. But that was false. Completely. No one can *do*. Things only happen, A and B are unreal, are names for parts that ought to be inseparable . . ." (30). This is less formal doctrine, on "this side," than felt recognition that everything is connected in a network sensitive to vibration at its furthest reaches, and is meant to undermine the distinctness of the waking consciousness that separates what is joined in the night. One night Kekulé dreamt the archetypal Great Serpent and the dream tripped his imagination to the fact that the benzene molecule has the shape of a ring; this created an aromatic chemistry and made possible the German dye industry which became I.G. Farben (financing surveillance of Baby Tyrone). The paranoid narrator views these connections as evidence of a sinister continuity: "So that the right material may find its way to the right dreamer, everyone, everything involved must be exactly in place in the pattern. It was nice of Jung to give us the idea of an ancestral pool in which everybody shares the same dream material. But how is it we are each visited as individuals, each by exactly and only what he needs? Doesn't that imply a switching-path of some kind? a bureaucracy?" (410).

Jung's ancestral pool claims that consciousness is but an "island in the ocean" of the "psyche." Pynchon's appropriation of that notion helps imply a universe less particled and more whole, but one possibly more controlled than we are in the habit of admitting. Jung asserts that "since modern research has acquainted us with the fact that individual consciousness is based on and surrounded by an indefinitely extended psyche, we must needs revise our somewhat old-fashioned prejudice that man is nothing but his consciousness."[6]

Archetypes are symbolic keys to the "collective unconscious" we all share. The archetypal symbol Jung kept running into throughout his career was the "mandala." He knew of the mandala's significance in Tibetan Buddhism and in medieval religious art (where its form structures paintings of the Heavenly City), but he was fascinated by its frequent recurrence in the dreams of his patients, who knew nothing of the symbol's ubiquity. "Mandala" in Sanskrit means "circle," and the elements of its symbolism that Jung documented are these:

1. *Circular, spherical,* or *egg-shaped* formation.
2. The circle is elaborated into a *flower* (rose, lotus) or a *wheel.*
3. A centre expressed by a *sun, star,* or *cross,* usually with four, eight, or twelve rays.
4. The circles, spheres, and cruciform figures are represented in *rotation* (swastika).
5. The circle is represented by a *snake* coiled about a centre, either ring-shaped (uroboros) or spiral (Orphic egg).
6. *Squaring of the circle,* taking the form of a circle in a square or vice versa.
7. *Castle, city,* and *courtyard (temenos)* motifs, quadratic or circular.
8. *Eye* (pupil and iris).
9. Besides the tetradic figures (and multiples of four), there are also triadic and pentadic ones, though these are much rarer.[7]

According to Francis Yates, mandala forms also underlay the structure of the Globe Theatre.[8] Yates traces the cosmogonic architecture of the Elizabethan stage as intentional microcosm of the heavens; thus Shakespeare's "all the world's a stage" has, like Pynchon's "it's all theatre," a literal basis. The Globe's sphericity, however, is replaced in *Gravity's Rainbow* by the Orphic disintegrations of the Orpheus Theatre, in which we sit at the novel's close.

The mandala symbols which pervade the Zone of *Gravity's Rainbow* are meant to invoke an integrating force which spars with the disintegrating forces of analysis, and is itself a symbol capable of uniting both (as it unites all opposition). Kekulé's Great Serpent is the mandalic version of the carbon cycle, made up of molecules whose tetravalency is symbolized by the cross:

The mandala's social and political implications are established by Andreas Orukambe, when he explains to Tyrone the meaning of the V-2 emblem Slothrop had found:

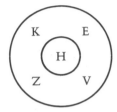

Andreas sets it on the ground, turns it till the K points northwest. "Klar,"
touching each letter, "Entlüftung, these are the female letters. North
letters. In our villages the women lived in huts on the northern half of
the circle, the men on the south. The village itself was a mandala. Klar is
fertilization and birth, Entlüftung is the breath, the soul. Zündung and
Vorstufe are the male signs, the activities, fire and preparation or building. And in the center here, Hauptstufe. It is the pen where we kept the
sacred cattle. The souls of the ancestors. All the same here. Birth, soul,
fire, building. Male and female, together.

"The four fins of the Rocket made a cross, another mandala. Number
one pointed the way it would fly. Two for pitch, three for yaw and roll,
four for pitch. Each opposite pair of vanes worked together, and moved in
opposite senses. Opposites together. You can see how we might feel it
speak to us, even if we don't set one up on its fins and worship it. . . ."
(563)

Pynchon knows his Herero language and culture (see below, pp.
83–88).[9] The Zone-Hereros are a rationalized people still sensitive to structural echoes of their former tribal cosmology. The
mandala, throughout *Gravity's Rainbow*, exists as a symbol for a
unified sensibility fragmented by the western European habit of
understanding something by taking it apart.

Pynchon's social mandalas cover both sides of the Atlantic and
both hemispheres of the world and this recurrence is itself a
mandala. The Kazakh peoples Tchitcherine and Džaqyp Qulan
visit "are gathered in a circle" watching an "ajtys" or singing-
duel. The "boy and girl stand in the eye of the village" (356), while
ten years later the Russian looks down upon the Argentinians,
expatriated from citied Buenos Aires to the temporarily open
Zone of postwar Germany: "Townspeople are gathered in a circle,
but these Tchitcherine can crop out, leaving in his elliptical field
a scene with the same structures as the male-female singing con-

test in the middle of a flat grassland in Central Asia well over a decade ago—a coming together of opposites that signaled then his own approach to the Kirghiz Light. What does it signal this time?" (610).

All these mandalas have been broken: the Herero population was decimated by the Germans in 1904 and 1922; the Kazakhs were brutally incorporated into Stalin's communism in the 1920s (the introduction of the new Turkic alphabet is pointed evidence of Levi-Strauss's hypothesis that "the primary function of written communication is to facilitate slavery");[10] and the Argentinians are acting out the celluloid hope von Göll has given them. Jung is quick to point out that mandalas, particularly modern expressions of them, are therapeutic: "they often follow chaotic, disordered states marked by conflict and anxiety. They express the idea of a safe refuge, of inner reconciliation and wholeness."[11]

The mandala is a visionary image of reality in which its parts are united, though this same reality is experienced as multiplicity, and unity remains a doubtful and ominous possibility. The mandala formed by the integration of Tyrone's and Mexico's maps is the most important example in the book of this paradox, but Mexico himself, one December morning, manages a momentary bonding of the two realities, as his map of London catches him: "red pockmarks on the pure white skin of lady London, watching over all . . . *wait* . . . disease on skin . . . *does* she carry the fatal infection inside herself? are the sites predestined, and does the flight of the rocket actually follow from the fated eruption *latent in the city*" (125). The presence of this vision is implied in Leni Pokler's efforts to map "onto different coordinate systems"; after watching *Die Frau im Mond*, she echoes Roland Feldspath: Leni "saw a dream of flight. One of many possible. Real flight and dreams of flight go together. Both are part of the same movement. Not A before B, but all together" (159).

The "latent" mandala these characters glimpse is not the structure of salvation. The mandala in *Gravity's Rainbow* is not an image of a realm transcending our own but one which represents the integration of conflicts within the realm. Thus the Raketen-Stadt, or Rocket-City, is also in the shape of a mandala (725), even though the city for Pynchon is "the desert in disguise" (*V.,* 71), and the "Vertical Solution" (735) the city represents is the illusion that society can save. As the "Revealer," showing that "no society can protect," the Rocket is an instrument of integration (728). The mandala of the Rocket state–cosmology embraces both life and death but is a transcendence of neither. It does "transcend" the sterile and divisive presumption of civilization— "To keep us worse than enemies, who are all caught in the same fields of shit—to keep us strangers" (739)—that it could distinguish life and save us from death. As such the mandala is party to Pynchon's project of redefining the all-at-once inextricability of events congruent with the one-way time of historical causation. It is possible, even, to construct a map of Pynchon's mandalas (see the accompanying figure). This map is not the structure of *Gravity's Rainbow* but a synthesis of the recurring and implied secular continuity within which his characters must live.

The disintegrations which, paradoxically, comprise that continuity require little documentation. Tyrone is disassembled; *Gravity's Rainbow* itself from this vantage seems to scatter. But this is part of Pynchon's description of a disposition no longer capable of acting out of the intersections it inhabits. Pynchon's use of signs to read social history finds its way into this conversation between Sir Stephen Dodson-Truck and Slothrop, who is confused by the symbol for "coil" in German schematics:

". . . that coil symbol there happens to be very like the Old Norse rune for 'S,' *sôl*, which means 'sun.' The Old High German for it is *sigil*."

"Funny way to draw that *sun*," it seems to Slothrop.

"Indeed. The Goths, much earlier, had used a circle with a dot in the center. This broken line evidently dates from a time of discontinuities, tribal fragmenting perhaps, alienation—whatever's analogous, in a social sense, to the development of an independent ego by the very young child, you see. . . ." (206)

Dodson-Truck's analysis is linked to the "primacy of the 'conscious' self" and emphasizes an ambiguity which surrounds the concept of integration in *Gravity's Rainbow:* the independence of the ego—its integration—is at the same time a disintegration, separating the self from other types of continuity.

This brief social etymology continues to reverberate as the broken rune bears out its heritage in the coils of the A-4 (V-2). These coils tell the rocket when to shut off its burning (*Brennschluss*).

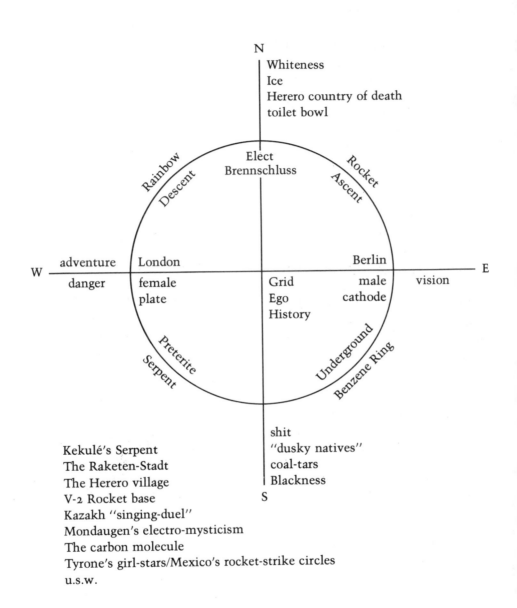

Pynchon's Mandalas

This requires a double integration, the symbol for which is an elongated double "S" or SS. For the engineer Ölsch, the rocket by double integration achieves a timeless stasis, as the equations remove duration ("per second") from distance ("meters"). This is an engineer's way of avoiding change (a theme anticipated by Oedipa's realization that "velocity dwelled in the projectile though the projectile be frozen in midflight").

But the "double integral is also the shape of two lovers curled asleep," Katje/Tyrone, female and male united. The voice of *Gravity's Rainbow* gives different meanings to the same signs; this ambiguity—as Pokler discovered—forces upon us the act of making a choice. Which is real? Which do you want it to be? These difficult pages on the double integral (300–302) have to do with the choice and values implicit in the reading of signs. For Ölsch and "some corrupted idea of 'Civilization'" (the Third Reich), the double integral locates a center which is thought of not as "heart" or "consciousness" (living, sentient) but as a "point in space ... where the burning must end" (302). For the Pathetic Fallacy, science substitutes abstract constellations whose stars exist only on paper.

Max Weber and the "disenchantment of the world"

> Director Carl Denham announced to his New York audience: " I want you to see the greatest thing your eyes have ever beheld. He was a king and a god in the world he knew, but now he comes to civilization merely a captive, a show to gratify your curiosity. Look at Kong, the eighth wonder of the world!"
>
> *King Kong* (1933)[12]

In his lecture "Science as a Vocation," Weber uses Friedrich Schiller's phrase: "The fate of our times is characterized by rationalization and intellectualization and, above all, by the 'disenchantment of the world.'"[13] For Weber, the progressive secular rationalization of the world is a theory of history. Jung uses the phrase "despiritualization of the world." In *The Theory of Social and Economic Organization* Weber outlines the two forces which shape his view of history. "Charisma" is one of the three pure types of legitimate authority (beside rational and traditional) and carries with it no valuation, but throughout his writings the concept allies itself with love, freedom, brotherhood, and an indifference to economic considerations. However, "in its pure form charismatic authority may be said to exist only in the process of originating. It cannot remain stable, but becomes either traditionalized or rationalized, or a combination of both."[14] Weber called this the "routinization of charisma"—the phrase Andreas Orukambe uses to describe what had happened to Enzian since his first days in Europe (325).

The most stable form of government is "the purely bureaucratic type of administrative organization." This type is the most "rational known means of carrying out imperative control over human beings. It is superior to any other form in precision, in stability, in the stringency of its discipline, and in its reliability."[15] Clustered around "bureaucracy"—the dialectical opposite of "charisma"—we find these elements: impersonality, an abstract currency, and the rational state modeled after the corporations of modern capitalism.

Weber's concept of rationalization penetrates every sphere of human activity. He even wrote a book about the *Rational Foundations of Music.* In the efficient economy "the development of the *money economy,* in so far as a pecuniary compensation of the officials is concerned, is a presupposition of bureaucracy," but he points out in "Religious Rejections of the World and Their Directions" that money is "the most abstract and 'impersonal' element that exists in human life."[16] In addition, the absence of love is characteristic of those religions which are "rational." Weber calls these the "salvation" religions; his test case is *The Protestant Ethic and the Spirit of Capitalism.* The vocabulary of that book ("grace," "invisibility," "elect," "loneliness") should be aligned with its context in the Church of England's *Book of Common Prayer;* together they are the matrix for the meanings of those words in *Gravity's Rainbow,* especially as they apply to the "Progress" of the modern Puritan, Tyrone Slothrop.

Weber's influence is pervasive; it dominates the very processes of human activity in *Gravity's Rainbow,* as well as the process of the book itself. The movement from charisma to the consolidations of power in rational bureaucracies may be said to be the Force against which the other, less-organized "enclaves" of affirmation must struggle.[17]

Pynchon uses Weber partly for purposes of historical verisimilitude. Charisma, in the shape of the Führer principle, created one of the "dearest Postwar hopes: that there should be no room for a terrible disease like charisma . . . that its rationalization should proceed while we had the time and resources" (GR, 81). And one of the voices from the other side is Walter Rathenau, German industrialist and financier, "the architect of the cartelized state" who saw rising out of the War "a rational structure in which business would be the true, the rightful authority" (164–65).

Weber's model is also the controlling structure which governs Gravity's Rainbow's dramatic history. The period of the war represents a temporal charisma. Weber pinpointed times of distress and chaos as seedbeds of charisma. Pynchon shows how the war weakens control so that its machinery becomes visible. Anarchist Squalidozzi comes to Germany because the War "just for the moment has wiped out the proliferation of little states that's prevailed in Germany for a thousand years. Wiped it clean. Opened it" (265); black marketeer Schnorp assures Slothrop that there are "no zones but the Zone" (333); and later it occurs to Tyrone that Squalidozzi may be right, and that this post-War moment is like the "singular point" America "jumped the wrong way from" long ago when her spaces were open (556).

Soon, however, the White Market reasserts its controls (570), the Zone is divided into British, Soviet, and American consolidations, and Enzian's enterprise must find its freedom along the interface of political boundaries (731). The dialectics of routinization undermine even the Counterforce, who had resolved: "The dearest nation of all is one that will survive no longer than you and I, a common movement at the mercy of death and time: the ad hoc adventure" (706). The Counterforce, which goes into the Zone looking for Slothrop, is consciously disorganized. This bothers Mexico, but Osbie Feel screams, "That's exactly it. . . . They're the rational ones. We piss on Their rational arrangements. Don't we . . . Mexico?" (639).

Pirate Prentice seems to be aware that their efforts are doomed from the beginning. What he tells Mexico is extremely important to any reading of *Gravity's Rainbow*, because it undermines the temptation to read the book as a Manichean allegory. Mexico's initial reflex, once he realizes that Pointsman is behind Jessica's disappearance, is to divide the world into Them against Us, and to understand all hostile events as emanations from Them. But Pirate sets him straight: "'You're a novice paranoid, Roger,' first time Prentice has ever used his Christian name and it touches Roger enough to check his tirade. 'Of course a well-developed They-system is necessary—but it's only half the story. For every They there ought to be a We. In our case there is....'" This sounds simple enough, but what Pirate means by They and We systems are "delusional systems" which have the virtue of "expediency." This troubles Roger; he wants a We system that is real and righteous: "Well, you're playing Their game, then." Prentice is unruffled: "Don't let it bother you.... Seeing as we haven't won yet, it isn't really much of a problem" (638).

Pirate's expediency underlines the melancholy whimsy of the entire book. The reader, like Mexico, wants to take the Counterforce seriously, join in the movement against oppression, and ride the wave to the end of the book and a happy resolution. Instead, Pynchon undermines his boobish heroes ("Double-de-clutchingly, heel-and-toe, away goes Roger Mexico") and mimics them in a comic-book sequence in which Tyrone is one of the Floundering Four fighting the Father Conspiracy and the System's "iceboxery: freezing back the tumultuous cycles of the day to preserve this odorless small world, this cube of changelessness" (678): "Any wonder it's hard to feel much confidence in these idiots as they go up against Pernicious Pop each day? There's no real direction here, neither lines of power nor cooperation. Decisions are never really *made*—at best they manage to emerge, from a chaos of peeves, whims, hallucinations and all-around assholery" (676). Tyrone can't even keep himself out of "Iceboxland" (677), an oblique reprise of that London icebox "stale-smelling and no surprises inside" where he found the little girl, long ago.

Tyrone's addiction to sweets is another impurity of the Counterforce; part of what they fight is inside themselves. When Bo-

dine and Mexico are invited to the Utgarthaloki dinner party
("the bosom of the Opposition"), the narrator reminds us of
Oedipa's rage on the California freeways: "the Man has a branch
office in each of our brains. . . . We do know what's going on, and
we let it go on" (712–13). The Counterforce achieves a temporary
victory against the Force that night. Mexico and Bodine (in his
"*paint*-blue" zoot suit) break up the party by violating linguistic
decorum, and Bodine feels "high in the good chances of death"
(715). That Maileresque passage (compare Mailer before the mar-
shals in *Armies of the Night*) reminds us that the price of not
letting it go on is death, that any compromise is a "decision to
live, on Their terms" (713). As the name of the host indicates
("Utgarthaloki" is the name of the Norse Titan chief who crosses
over the rainbow bridge Bifrost and storms Asgard, abode of the
gods), their victory is temporary. By the end of the book, the
Counterforce has become legitimate, as evidenced by the phony
double-talk of its bureaucratized spokesman. Tyrone, the initial
object of their quest, has become only a "pretext" or "microcosm": "We were never that concerned with Slothrop *qua* Slothrop" (738).

The Counterforce is co-opted; the "revolutionaries of May"
turn into the white crystals of winter; children become adults.

Gravity's Rainbow does provide some examples of a power
which resists stabilization. The stories of Mexico's love for Jessica, and of Geli's for Tchitcherine, are guided by the oppositions
Weber established between the magic of love and the routine of
bureaucracy. At the end of Part 1 Roger begins to feel how easily
Jessica might return to her pre-War love, the stuffy Jeremy:

If the rockets don't get her there's still her lieutenant. Damned
Beaver/Jeremy *is* the War, he is every assertion the fucking War has ever
made—that we are meant for work and government, for austerity: and
these shall take priority over love, dreams, the spirit, the senses and the
other second-class trivia that are found among the idle and mindless
hours of the day. . . . Damn them, they are wrong. They are insane. (177)

Love establishes a home in the Creation. It integrates: Jessica and
Roger are "merged into a joint creature unaware of itself." For
him this is something new: "In a life he has cursed, again and

again, for its need to believe so much in the trans-observable, here is the first, the very first real magic: data he can't argue away" (38).

The magic between Roger and Jessica has something to do with love, and love has something to do with a sense of connection, of being part of something or somebody else. This sense of connection is in part a realization that the real facts are precisely trans-observable, perhaps not in the way which Psi-section hopes to find them (measurable, detectable), but as all social facts are trans-observable. Love is the highest expression of this social continuity, where humans find something in their union which transcends their individualities, is more real and more important than themselves separately, and which redeems their separateness, returning it to the world of dream, love, and joy. As Roger meditates on the brink of losing Jessica, the prose exhibits the fusion he himself is experiencing, as reader, character, and narrator are molded into a declension of personal pronouns: "You go from dream to dream inside me. You have passage to my last shabby corner, and there, among the debris, you've found life. I'm no longer sure which of all the words, images, dreams or ghosts are 'yours' and which are 'mine.' It's past sorting out. We're both being someone new now, someone incredible . . ." (176). As is always the case with Pynchon, his entire fiction works against such precarious moments. The book itself seeks to destroy the hopefulness of its author and reader—not to deny love but to dramatize its poor chances among the power bureaucracies of control and separation.

The relationship between love and magic is further defined by Geli Tripping's search for Tchitcherine. When she consults an experienced witch, Geli admits she isn't very good at some of the spells; the old pro assures her, "But you're in love. Technique is just a substitute for when you get older" (718). Immediately following this piece of dialogue, Pynchon divides magic itself into two types, making as clear a Weberian expression of the charisma/bureaucracy model as we find in the book:

The Hexes-Stadt, with its holy mountains cropped in pale circles all up and down their green faces by the little tethered goats, has turned into just another capital, where the only enterprise is administrating—the feeling there is of upstairs at the musicians' union—no music, just glass-brick partitions, spittoons, indoor plants—no *practicing* witches left. You either come to the Brocken-complex with a bureaucratic career in mind, or you leave it, and choose the world. There are two distinct sorts of witch, and Geli is the World-choosing sort. (718)

Geli gets her man, not because she invokes the names of the Kabbala's angel-hierarchy (734) but because she loves Tchitcherine, because her relationship to him is the most important reality of her life, and because she goes into the Zone looking for him. "He takes the bread now. The stream rushes. A bird sings." There are moments of peace such as this in *Gravity's Rainbow*, where the prose itself relaxes, and it is a sign from the Storyteller that all is well, at least here and now, for these two. As God of this universe, Pynchon has spared them, a measure of both the difficulty and possibility of love in this world.

The moment—as origin of charismatic freedom—stabilizes into the bureaucracy of time. In the face of uncertainty, people seek control. Pynchon reserves some of his bitterest reproach for those who acquiesce to the forms that obscure the terror of the moment. From the beginning of *Gravity's Rainbow* characters perceive their experiences through forms. The girl's Shirley Temple smile mitigates for Tyrone the desolation in which he finds her; Pointsman tries to understand all behavior using only Pavlov's mechanical model; Blicero, Katje, and Gottfried retreat into the formal security of *Hansel and Gretel*. Experience is thereby reduced to a reflection of the forms we project upon it. At the end of "Shit'N'Shinola" the narrator speculates: "did Red suspend his ragpopping just the shadow of a beat, just enough gap in the moiré there to let white Jack see through, not through to but through *through* the shine on his classmate Tyrone Slothrop's shoes?" (688). Might Kennedy have seen beyond the pornography of motion to the true continuity?

There is no question about Pynchon's attitude toward the reduction of experience. Katje joins Blicero in his game because she feels it is better "to enter into some formal, rationalized version of what, outside, proceeds without form or decent limit." *Hansel and Gretel*, "this Northern and ancient form, . . . shall be their preserving routine, their shelter, against what outside none of them can bear—the War, the absolute rule of chance, their own

pitiable contingency here, in its midst . . ." (96). On the other side
of the channel, giving resonance to Part 1, is an ironic reprise:
Roger and Jessica take the nieces to see a pantomime of *Hansel
and Gretel*. What is this fairy tale but the story of children (mankind), left (by the parents) to stray into the forest (of life), and who
manage like Dorothy to burn the witch (death/Pernicious Pop)
and escape. It is not much different, finally, from *The Wizard of
Oz*. Pynchon interrupts this pantomime, however, with a rocket
strike down the street; Gretel steps out to calm the children and
begins a song, "Oh, don't let it get you," but the song ends
"(Whispered and staccato)"

> And those voices you hear, Boy and Girl of the Year,
> Are of children who are learning to die. . . . (175)

Pynchon is equally clear about those who live under the as-
sumption of a personal destiny. Leni leaves Franz precisely because of his passive submission to what is given; she has him
figured out: "Destiny will betray you, crush your ideals, deliver
you into the same detestable Bürgerlichkeit as your father, suck-
ing at his pipe on Sunday strolls after church past the row houses
by the river—dress you in the gray uniform of another family
man, and without a whimper you will serve out your time, fly
from pain to duty, from joy to work, from commitment to neu-
trality. Destiny does all this to you" (162). Early in the 1930s
Pokler loses his wife Leni and daughter Ilse. It isn't until ten years
later, while occupying a barrack in Germany's losing war effort,
that he understands how much he misses them. Every summer
Pokler is sent a girl who claims to be his daughter. In one of the
most moving events in the book we find Pokler at Zwolfkinder (a
children's resort) still waiting for "Ilse." Pynchon begins the
Pokler chapter (397–433) with that picture, a ferris wheel in the
background, "stars hang among the spaces of the great Wheel,
precarious as candles and good-night cigarettes" (398). Stars and
wheels have lost their connection; we don't even hear of Pokler
again for another hundred and fifty pages. When Slothrop finds
him, Franz is still waiting; the narrative gap underlines his desolation and loneliness. We had forgotten him, hadn't we? Wind
blows through the spaces of the park, and Zwolfkinder's model of
Hansel and Gretel has fallen into disrepair: "The plaster witch,

wire mesh visible at her breasts, and haunches, leans near the oven, her poke at corroded Hansel in perpetual arrest. Gretel's eyes lock wide open, never a blink, crystal-heavy lashes batting at the landings of guerrilla winds from the sea" (398). The fairy tale hasn't worked for anyone; the chapter ends with Pokler's visit to Camp Dora, which, at the same time that Franz had been in the service of the Rocket, had been using the imagery of the "Northern and ancient form" to teach children how to die.

For Pynchon the rationalization of experience coded in fairy tales and myths has the serious consequences implied in his *Hansel and Gretel* motif. Unlike Jung's symbols of the unconscious, these rationalizations repress and destroy experience; Pynchon uses Jung to emphasize orders which inhere in experience. He knows that his own book—any writing, any system—is by contrast a "projection, *onto*" experience. Much of his narrative, as a result, is self-consciously ironic:

It's a Rocket-raising: a festival new to this country. Soon it will come to the folk-attention how close Wernher von Braun's birthday is to the Spring Equinox, and the same German impulse that once rolled flower-boats through the towns and staged mock battles between young Spring and deathwhite old Winter will be erecting strange floral towers out in the clearings and meadows, and the young scientist-surrogate will be going round and round with old Gravity or some such buffoon, and the children will be tickled, and laugh. (361)

The workers in the Mittelwerke are described as "post A-4 humanity" (304); the Rocket has destroyed the old European order (551) and has inaugurated a "new dispensation brought into being by the Great Firing" (753).

Not that within the context of the book this isn't true enough. Enzian realizes that the Rocket has come as "the Revealer. Showing that no society can protect, never could . . . the Rocket can penetrate, from the sky, at any given point. Nowhere is safe" (728). Enzian's exegesis is a fundamental theme of *Gravity's Rainbow*, but the apotheosis of the V-2 Pynchon treats with irony. The rocket so conceived is a transformation of a man-made weapon into an instrument of divine will. As the book hurtles towards its last delta-t, therefore, Pynchon places Gottfried's ascension in numerous mythic, religious, and popular forms.

Sometime before the final day Gottfried has failed to seize the
moment of Blicero's uncertainty: "It all poises here. Passageways
of routine, still cogent enough, still herding us through time . . .
the iron rockets waiting outside. . . . If there is still hope for
Gottfried here in this wind-beat moment, then there is hope
elsewhere. The scene itself must be read as a card: what is to
come" (724). That is the theme of these closing pages: "What will
come: The World" (747). Pynchon reads the past like a Tarot deck,
using as metaphor a mysticism he parodies. The firing and the
men involved are transformed by the text of *Gravity's Rainbow*
into archetypes of Kabbalistic tradition and cards of the Tarot; the
lift-off is a "Sacrifice," which mocks their ignorance. In "Isaac"
the prototype of last-minute salvation is invoked, but the "ascent
to the Merkabah . . . is irreversibly on route" (750). All this is
irony. In "Chase Music" Sir Nayland Smith, Philip Marlowe, the
Lone Ranger, and Superman all arrive too late. Throughout, the
narrator maintains his distance from these transformations; his
qualifying disdain keeps always before us the actual nature of the
singular event: "But no, the ritual has its velvet grip on them
all" (758). The "first star" (760) hanging between Gottfried's feet
grants no wishes, for it is the Rocket's fire carrying him to
Brennschluss, and the fall beyond.

"Which do you want it to be?"

Working against such paralyzing ritual is a question which structures the Advent scene Roger and Jessica attend: "Which do you
want it to be?" Listening to the night's "scratch choir" singing
evensong, Jessica glances sideways at Roger's face, which for once
"wasn't looking nihilistic." It seems to her that his skin is "more
child-pink, his eyes more glowing than the lamp-light alone can
account for—isn't it? or is that how she wants it to be?" (129).
This is the beginning of a fine scene filled with bitter, elegiac
compassion in which the narrator sings his own "War's evensong"—his words going out over the English countryside, to
London and the channel beaches buried in fog. At one point we
lean over the "infant prince"—the narrator's song parodies Advent imagery—and the question this time is addressed to us: "Is

the baby smiling, or is it just gas? Which do you want it to be?"
(131). The War, for Pynchon, is all those forces which claim our
"belief in so much that isn't true"—including the redeeming
power of the Child. His reach is inclusive: "Everybody you don't
suspect is in on this... let's not forget Mr. Noel Coward so
stylish and cute about death and the afterlife, packing them into
the Duchess for the fourth year running," and "Walt Disney
causing Dumbo the elephant to clutch to that feather like how
many carcasses under the snow tonight among the white-painted
tanks, how many hands each frozen around a Miraculous Medal,
lucky piece of worn bone, half-dollar with the grinning sun peer-
ing up under Liberty's wispy gown, clutching, dumb, when the 88
fell—what do you think, it's a children's story? There aren't any"
(135).

Movies, myths, musicals, and children's stories all reveal the
human reflex for hope (how easily it comes), and the sickness of
our willingness to wait in the night. In this passage through War's
evensong the narrator returns to those leaving the church tonight,
imparting to them (and us) the curiously intimate power of the
second person: "But on the way home tonight, you wish you'd
picked him up, held him a bit, very close to your heart, his cheek
by the hollow of your shoulder, full of sleep. As if it were you who
could, somehow, save him." These are hints of another world, in
which people do not seek salvation from the newly born but show
one another mercy instead. For all we have, sings Pynchon's
evensong, is "the path you must create by yourself, alone in the
dark. Whether you want it or not, whatever seas you have crossed,
the way home . . ." (136).

One of Pynchon's metaphors for this dark and lonely freedom is
the "singular point." The entire rhetorical push of Gravity's
Rainbow may be felt as Pynchon's effort to take us to that point,
just as in V. we are left in the "real present" and with Oedipa in
the "excluded middle." Singularities are specific mathematical
events.[18] What Pynchon means by them (as with almost all his
important metaphors drawn from science) is sufficiently clear
from the text of the book. His examples are drawn from the world
of experience: the top of a lady's stocking, a cathedral spire, the
edges of a steel razor. These points have several characteristics in
common: they are points of transition (silk to bare skin, spire to

sky, steel to what it cuts), "always holding potent mystery. . . . In each case, the change from point to no-point carries a luminosity and enigma at which something in us must leap and sing or withdraw in fright" (396).

The concept is allied to "cusps," which is why the book attaches so much importance to the "great cusp" of green equinox (236). This is a time of change, of bursting forth, and a point of maximum freedom. A cusp, any cusp, is that point formed by the intersection of two or more curves. The "cusp of the moon" is thus formed; at the cusp is the "singular point." Tyrone wonders if his ancestor could have been "the fork in the road America never took, the singular point she jumped the wrong way from" (556). In the vernacular of *Gravity's Rainbow* all lives are a succession of such points, where the curves of history form the terrible intersection from which we must choose a direction.

Most of the characters in *Gravity's Rainbow* "withdraw in fright." The price of their withdrawal is clear: "So generation after generation of men in love with pain and passivity serve out their time in the Zone, silent, redolent of faded sperm, terrified of dying, desperately addicted to the comforts others sell them, however useless, ugly or shallow, willing to have life defined for them by men whose only talent is for death" (747). In this way the book reminds us of Silvernail's "guest performance" (230), Pokler's movement from "joy to work" (162), and Jessica's defection from mindless love to the false safety of the System (176).

As Enzian knew, that System cannot save. Weissmann is "covered" by the Tower, a puzzling card which some generalize "to mean any System which cannot tolerate heresy: a system which, by its nature, must sooner or later fall. We know by now that it is also the Rocket" (747). The Rocket, as an "entire system *won,* away from the feminine darkness" (324), will nonetheless fall, a partial allegory buried in the rocket's symbolism, and bearing out the narrator's prophecy in the Kekulé section: "The System may or may not understand that it's only buying time. And that time is an artificial resource to begin with, of no value to anyone or anything but the System, which sooner or later must crash to its death, when its addiction to energy has become more than the rest of the World can supply" (412). By the end of *Gravity's Rainbow* such prophecy is almost welcome, until we remember that we—like Mexico—are part of the system. And this is why the book ends with the singular point of the Rocket poised above our heads, instead of having some Ishmael crawl up out of the rubble.

The ground against which this singular freedom is urged is a molecular mindlessness. The essential mindlessness of the universe is a theme in Sidney Stencil's journal, and has its most complete expression in Fausto Maijstral's diary entry about poets, who "are alone with the task of living in a universe of things which simply are, and cloaking that innate mindlessness with comfortable and pious metaphor so that the 'practical' half of humanity may continue in the Great Lie" (V., 305). Roger Mexico opposes the "mindless trivia" of love and dreams to war and government, but the participants at Nürnberg are "mostly brains ravaged by antisocial and mindless pleasures" (681). The title of *Gravity's Rainbow* in an early Viking ad in *Publisher's Weekly* was "Mindless Pleasures."

The origin of this theme in *Gravity's Rainbow* is the seance in which Roland Feldspath, via Eventyr, tells us, "Once transected into the realm of Dominus Blicero, Roland found that all the signs had turned against him. . . . Lights he had studied so well as one of you, position and movement, now gathered there at the opposite end, all in dance . . . irrelevant dance" (30). Position and movement are the ways we locate things in space and time, a distinction absent in the continuum. This had been germane to Roland's expertise, for on This Side he had been an "expert on control systems, guidance equations, feedback situations" (238). Now, on the Other Side, he experiences the fact that what we attempt to measure over here as separate qualities are actually joined: "Things only happen, A and B are unreal, are names for parts that ought to be inseparable . . ." (30).

This becomes problematic, for already a kind of positive valuation becomes attached to this "dance"—if only because we are being told this is the nature of things. Feldspath's metaphor finds its way into several explanations of events. Wimpe thinks of chemistry as a chess game with "dance-figures in three-dimensions"; Tchitcherine is like a "giant molecule" to whom others, "in the dance of things . . . latch on" (346); the story of Lyle Bland's demise evolves from such mindless causation: "Just as there are, in the World, machineries committed to injustice as an enterprise, so too there seem to be provisions active for balancing things out once in a while. Not as an enterprise, exactly, but at least in the dance of things. The Masons, in the dance of things, turned out to be one of these where Bland was concerned" (580). Leni's dream for Ilse, we are told, will come true, one of the "accidents of the drifting Humility" (610).

Like Stencil's "Situation," it is the "cross-purposes" that are real. *Gravity's Rainbow*, as a structure, imitates the intersections of mindless dance and conscious enterprise. The entire book seems to oscillate between uncategorical assertions such as "the real and only fucking is done on paper" (616) and the love Geli and Vaslav manage under the bridge (734). "There are two sorts of movement out here," Peter Sachsa learns, losing Leni in the crowd just before his death—"as often as the chance displacements of strangers, across a clear skirmish-line from the Force, will bring together people who'll remain that way for a time, in love that can even make the oppression seem a failure, so too love, here in the street, can be taken centrifugally apart again" (219). Singular points exhort us to freedom and choice. Leni and the narrator indict Franz for lacking "commitment," yet human activity apparently occurs within a mindless dance of "chance displacements." When Tyrone witnesses the rainbow, "not a thing in his head, just feeling natural" (626), has he achieved some kind of rapprochement with the "innate mindlessness" of nature, or is it "one more negligence"?[19]

From Myth to Mathematics: The Orphic Pig as "delta-t"

The ambiguity of Tyrone's experience (rapprochement or negligence) is part of the same ambiguity surrounding the concept of integration mentioned earlier (p. 55). The independence of the ego is also the fragmentation of society and the cosmology binding it. This opposition is outlined in Mondaugen's "electro-mysticism":

Think of the ego, the self that suffers a personal history bound to time, as the grid. The deeper and true Self is the flow between cathode and plate. The constant, pure flow. Signals—sense-data, feelings, memories relocating—are put onto the grid, and modulate the flow. We live lives that are waveforms constantly changing with time, now positive, now negative. Only at moments of great serenity is it possible to find the pure, the informationless state of signal zero. (404)

Like Pokler, Tyrone lives in the "flow between cathode and plate"—"between the two desires, personal identity and impersonal salvation" (406). As Slothrop's search for his fake discharge papers becomes more futile, his "personal density" decreases and his existence in a pure present or "Now," oblivious to the past and the future, increases:

> "Uh," he turns slackmouth to Närrisch, "what are we . . ."
> "What are we what?"
> "What?"
> "You said, 'What are we . . . ,' then you stopped."
> "Oh. Gee, that was a funny thing to say." (509)

This comedy exemplifies how difficult Pynchon makes it for us to take the attenuation of the self seriously. In fact, this is much more problematic for readers than are the terms of his disappearance, which are themselves set forth clearly, though widely distributed and difficult to integrate.

Similarly, the vestments of the "Pig-Hero" are meant to associate Tyrone with the cyclical god Osiris, cousin of the Greek Orpheus, who, like the Adriatic harpman, is dismembered. In Egyptian mythology "the jackal-headed god Anubis . . . with the aid of Isis and Nephthys, of Thoth and Horus," piece together the dismembered god. Isis revives him with her wings.[20] Pynchon's use of such myth (as in *V.*) is never systematic, for it is both a parody of literary modernism and a serious invocation of mythic analogues within a "disenchanted" civilization. Frazer's research on "The Dying and Reviving Gods" is everywhere pertinent, but the following is especially intriguing: "after the examples of the goat Dionysus and the pig Demeter it may almost be laid down as a rule that an animal which is said to have injured a god was originally the god himself."[21] As in Oedipa's quest, Slothrop's search for Jamf and the papers of his historical identity carries with it an implicit self-destruction (*GR*, 287). This is not to agree with the fatuous Wuxtry-Wuxtry that Jamf never existed (738); Jamf represents outside of Tyrone an embodiment of The Man programed on Tyrone's "grid" inside, as Tristero is congruent with the surface of Oedipa's "cheered land."

Nature myth and Mondaugen's mysticism meet in Slothrop's Orphic fragmentation as he approaches the "delta-t" of his time-bound self. When he sees the graffiti, "ROCKETMAN WAS HERE," he thinks he may have written it himself: "Might be he was starting to implicate himself, some yesterday version of himself, in the Combination against who he was right then" (624). The possibility that his accumulated past selves, his "grid," are part of the conspiracy zeroing in on him never quite dawns on Tyrone; nor does he know that, "suckin' on his harp," he's "closer to being a spiritual medium than he's been yet" (622). The narrator glosses Tyrone's unconscious spiritualism with these lines from Rilke's *Sonnets to Orpheus:*

> And though Earthliness forget you,
> To the stilled Earth say: I flow.
> To the rushing water speak: I am.

Later, when Tyrone "becomes a cross himself," Pynchon is alluding to the preceding lines of Rilke's sonnet:

> Be Conversant with transformation.
> . . . .
> Be, in this immeasurable night,
> magic power at your senses' crossroad,
> be the meaning of their strange encounter.[22]

These lines represent an important thematic continuity in *Gravity's Rainbow*, initiated by the spirits from the Other Side of death, implicit in Mexico's statistical "angel's-eye view," and allied with the anti-City pastoralism both Rilke and Pynchon share.

The difficulty in trying to use these lines as an interpretative key to Slothrop's experience is that Tyrone's character cannot bear the weight of Rilke's poetry. This apparent contradiction between ideas and drama is characteristic of Pynchon's writing; that is, the dissonance between the idea-nexus Pynchon brings into play, and the dramatization of character within that nexus, means neither that Rilke is a red herring nor that Tyrone achieves Rilkean transcendence.

Tyrone does become "a living intersection" (625), but if this is a Rilkean event, it is necessarily without the joy attendant upon salvation; this salvation is "impersonal" and involves forsaking the very ego which wanted saving in the first place. In accordance with his mythic heritage, Tyrone is "broken down" and "scattered" (738); even Pig Bodine can't "hold him together" (740), though "some believe that fragments of Slothrop have grown into consistent personae of their own" (742).

The ambiguity surrounding Slothrop's Orphic passage, therefore, is built into *Gravity's Rainbow*. His "crossroads" experience has, like the Rocket, two vectors: one points toward the transcendental, the other toward death. His disappearance is both an "integration" (Rilke's "senses' crossroad," Jung's mandala) and a "disintegration" (Pavlov's "confusion of opposites," the breakdown of Weber's socially coherent self). Together the two form the mandala of Pynchon's Orpheus Theatre, which resurrects the scattered and scuffling god in the harmonica players who plague Zhlubb with the "silver chances of song."

Nothing much is made of this fragmentary survival, however, for that section ("Orpheus Puts Down Harp") ends with the scream of an air-raid siren announcing the arrival of the Rocket, which, in an adroit time loop, is just being launched in the next section, "The Clearing" (757). The Rocket's fall confirms Blicero's despair: *there is always the danger of falling* (723). His fear of falling is a fear of death, but one thing *Gravity's Rainbow* says clearly is that any hope for "song" in this world depends upon man's recognition of "life" and "death" as names for inseparable parts. Falling is the dominant movement of the book, from the opening pages in which SOE-quickened Prentice slides his cot beneath the falling Bloat (5), to the molecules which rearrange themselves around Gravity (590), to the ascent "betrayed to Gravity" (758) that closes the book. The Rocket, as dream of escape, is designed to fall. Insofar as Rilke disdains the machine and embraces death as the other half of perfect consciousness, his exhortations have a kind of normative weight for Pynchon, who seems to agree with these lines from *The Book of Hours:*

> [Man] must re-learn to fall, and resting
> patiently in sheer weight to lie,—
> he that with boasting's vain protesting
> swore he'd all winged fowl outfly.[23]

NOTES

1. From "Over the Rainbow," lyrics by E. Y. Harburg (New York: Leo Feist, Inc., 1967).

2. See *V-2*, trans. James Cleugh and Geoffrey Halliday (New York: Viking Press, 1958); and *Rockets, Missiles and Space Travel* (New York: Viking Press, 1958).

3. (New York: T. Yoseloff, 1959).

4. Max Weber, *The Theory of Social and Economic Organization*, trans. A. M. Henderson and Talcott Parsons (New York: Oxford University Press, 1947), p. 95.

5. *Sonnets to Orpheus*, trans. M. D. Herter Norton (New York: Norton Library, 1962), Sonnet 29, second part.

6. "The History and Psychology of a Natural Symbol," in *Psychology and Religion: West and East*, vol. 11 of *The Collected Works of C. G. Jung*, trans. R. F. C. Hull (Princeton, N.J.: Princeton University Press, 1969), p. 82.

7. "Concerning Mandala Symbolism," in *The Archetypes and the Collective Unconscious*, vol. 9 of *The Collected Works of C. G. Jung*, p. 361.

8. See *The Theatre of the World* (Chicago: University of Chicago Press, 1969).

9. Pynchon's use of the Herero culture has firm anthropological grounding. Levi-Strauss reports of a Bororo village that the "circular arrangement of the huts around the men's house is so important a factor in their social and religious life that the Salesian missionaries in the Rio das Garcas region were quick to realize that the surest way to convert the Bororo was to make them abandon their village in favor of one with houses set out in parallel rows." See *Triste Tropiques*, trans. John and Doreen Weightman (New York: Atheneum, 1975), pp. 220–21.

10. *Ibid.*, p. 299. This matter is discussed by Edward Mendelson in "Gravity's Encyclopedia," in *Mindful Pleasures*, ed. Levine and Leverenz, pp. 161–95.

11. "Concerning Mandala Symbolism," p. 384.

12. From Orville Goldner and George E. Turner, *The Making of King Kong* (New York: Barnes & Noble, 1975).

13. *From Max Weber: Essays in Sociology*, trans. and ed. H. H. Gerth and C. Wright Mills (New York: Oxford University Press, 1946), p. 155. In their introduction to Burckhardt's *The Civilization of the Renaissance in Italy* (New York: Harper Torchbooks, 1958), Benjamin Nelson and Charles Trinkaus group Weber with Burckhardt and Huizinga. The similarity they see among the three thinkers is highly suggestive for our reading of *Gravity's Rainbow* and the notions of "self" implied in the behavior of Slothrop: "Beneath their surfaces, *The Civilization of the Renaissance in Italy, The Waning of the*

Middle Ages, and *The Protestant Ethic and the Spirit of Capitalism* are variant versions of a common theme: Western man has irrevocably been cast out—has cast himself out—of a child-like world of enchantment and undividedness. Since the days of his exile (or was it withdrawal?) he has been wandering the world. Wherever he goes he is readily recognized since he bears a burden for everyone to see—the burden of selfhood" (pp. 18–19). See the discussion between Maijstral and Herbert Stencil in *V.*, where Maijstral answers Stencil's desire to exorcise Profane, " 'One would have to exorcise the city, the island, . . . the continents, the world. Or the western part. . . . We are western men' " (p. 424).

14. Weber, *The Theory,* p. 364.
15. *Ibid.,* p. 337.
16. *From Max Weber,* pp. 204, 331, 355.
17. Again, readers should turn to Mendelson's "Gravity's Encyclopedia" for further discussion of Weber's importance in Pynchon's writings.
18. For a more technical discussion of the "singular point," and one which reaches conclusions very different from my own, see Lance Ozier, "The Calculus of Transformation: More Mathematical Imagery in Gravity's Rainbow," *Twentieth Century Literature,* 21, no. 2 (May, 1975), 193–210.
19. This question is the basis or pivot of much controversy and interpretation regarding the implications of Slothrop's disappearance for the role of the "self" in the modern novel and changing views of what constitutes adequate character development. Lance Ozier interprets Tyrone's disappearance as a Rilkean transcendence. Joseph Slade, on the other hand, argues that Slothrop "is out of control, out of the karmic cycle, and out of touch with the world of men," in *Thomas Pynchon,* p. 210. Mendelson sees Pynchon's use of Tyrone as part of his "redefinition of character"—*Gravity's Rainbow*'s "single greatest technical achievement in the art of writing." See also Mark Siegel, *Creative Paranoia in Gravity's Rainbow* (New York: Kennikat Press, 1978), pp. 44–72, and William Plater, *The Grim Phoenix* (Bloomington: Indiana University Press, 1978), pp. 49, 97, 214–15.
20. Sir James George Frazer, *The New Golden Bough,* ed. Theodor H. Gaster (New York: Criterion Books, 1964), pp. 388–89.
21. *Ibid.,* p. 527.
22. Trans. M. D. Herter Norton.
23. Trans. A. L. Peck (London: Hogarth Press, 1961), p. 99.

Four

History and Fiction:
From Providence to Paranoia

> Only by taking an infinitesimally
> small unit for observation—the
> differentia of history, that is, the
> homogenous tendencies of men—
> and, attaining to the art of inte-
> grating them (taking the sums of
> these infinitesimals), can we hope
> to arrive at the laws of history.
>
> Leo Tolstoi, *War and Peace*

Tolstoi's historical calculus results in the integrations of *War and Peace*, a book as massive and reticulate as *Gravity's Rainbow*. The difference between them rests on Tolstoi's faith: "There is, and can be, no cause of an historical event save the one cause of all causes."[1] By contrast, Sidney Stencil's Situation exists "only in the minds of those who happened to be in on it at any specific moment," and these minds "tended to form a sum total or complex more mongrel than homogenous" (174). Pynchon's Situation is radically different from the cause-and-effect historicity of the nineteenth century, for Pynchon takes up where Henry Adams left off: staring into the twentieth century, bewildered by the multiplicity of a universe reduced "to a series of relations" to the self.[2] The narrator of *V.* translates: "People read what news they wanted to and each accordingly built his own rathouse of history's rags and straws" (209).

This devolution of unity to the "rathouses" created by individuals has its most extreme and rational expression in the psychosis of paranoia, in which the universe of multiplicity becomes a conspiracy organized around (and at) the self. Instances of such paranoia "bloom" in Pynchon's fiction: Mucho and Dr. Hilarius are examples in *The Crying of Lot 49*, as is Horst Achtfaden in *Gravity's Rainbow*. But this psychotic consciousness never fully overtakes the principal characters of Pynchon's fiction. They possess instead what Tantivy calls "operational paranoia" (25), which is more protective than psychotic and in which conspiracies have an actual if problematic basis in fact. All the major seekers balance on this operational ridge between disparate, literal facts and connected, overwhelming meaning. Stencil prays that he is not merely out to "exhume an hallucination"; Oedipa is either "in the orbiting ecstasy of a *true* paranoia" or is experiencing her relevance to America in "*some* paranoia" (italics mine, 137); *Gravity's Rainbow* oscillates between the paranoid "discovery that *everything is connected*" (703) and the equally disturbing possibility that nothing is connected. Both sides of this ridge are presented plausibly in Pynchon's fiction, for the reason that this ambiguity is the just mirror of our situational dilemma.

In each of Pynchon's books the search for meaning results in a quest for "history." This is the palpable fact of Stencil's chase, but is also the enlightening consequence of Oedipa's and Tyrone's more personal motivations. The resulting "histories" are part of the more general description in his fiction of man's effort to gain control by establishing meaning. Accordingly, Pynchon's "histories" lack the closed finish of a dogmatic thesis, just as his fiction stops short of the integration it implies. The histories that men write are a linguistic membrane between us and what really happened, but a tissue without which there would be no connection at all.

Of all Pynchon's early stories, "Under the Rose" most clearly establishes his preoccupation with history.[3] The setting for this drama of spy intrigue is the Upper Nile in 1898, and the political moment is recorded in official history as the Fashoda Crisis, the clash of the French and British in the Sudan that many feared would ignite a world war.

The "balloon" never goes up, but Pynchon's spy drama is a political version of the crisis of world-view associated with the end of the nineteenth century. The Fashoda incident is mere background for the truer history represented by the drama of opposing spy networks in the story. The chiefs of these networks (Porpentine of the British Foreign Office, and Moldweorp, the "veteran spy") are "comrade Machiavellians, still playing the games of Renaissance Italian politics in a world that had outgrown them." The story, in other words, marks the effacement of an older order: "spying was becoming less an individual than a group enterprise, where the events of 1848 and the activities of anarchists and radicals all over the Continent seemed to proclaim that history was being made no longer through the virtù of single princes but rather by man in the mass." The movement described here reminds us of both Ortega and Weber; their sociological analyses are linked by Porpentine's growing paranoia about the mathematical methodology mass movements require:

like a bright hallucination against Cairo's night-sky he saw (it may have been only a line of cloud) a bell-shaped curve, remembered perhaps from some younger F.O. operative's mathematics text. Unlike Constantine on the verge of battle, he could not afford, this late, to be converted at any sign. Only curse himself, silent, for wanting so to believe in a fight according to the duello, even in this period of history. But they—no, it—had not been playing those rules. Only statistical odds. When had he stopped facing an adversary and taken on a Force, a Quantity?[4]

Porpentine's despair in "Under the Rose" becomes Sidney Stencil's: "There were no more princes. Henceforth politics would become progressively more democratized, more thrown into the hands of amateurs" (V., 461).

The short story "Under the Rose" reappears in Pynchon's first novel as its third chapter, "In which Stencil, a quick-change artist, does eight impersonations" (50). The changes the story undergoes in its novelistic incorporation mark a development in narrative technique which shows Pynchon moving toward a method of story-telling that exemplifies what is being told. "Under the Rose" is straight third-person narration; while parts of it are typically Pynchonian in their compactness and density, they are, nonetheless, straightforward and linked in temporal succession. The reader has little difficulty distinguishing characters, discerning motivation, or discovering the action. By the time the story reaches V., all this has changed. The opposing leader of the "comrade Machiavellians," Moldweorp, is gone, transformed into the less specific and more malign presence of the mechanical Bongo-Shaftesbury (who was Moldweorp's subordinate in the short story). The entire theme of "gentlemanly" opposition represented so clearly by Porpentine and Moldweorp is obscured and made a motif in the novel. And the action of the story, as it appears in *V.*, is conveyed through eight "impersonations" of Herbert Stencil, and is therefore questionable and elusive.

Stencil is on a quest initiated by this cryptic note in his father's journals: "There is more behind and inside V. than any of us had suspected" (43). Like Oedipa after him, all Stencil has are words, "the veiled references to Porpentine in the journals. The rest was impersonation and dream" (52). Pursuit, as we have said, animates Stencil, but he discovers (and ignores) eventually that V. is the very principle of Inanimateness. The quest is salutary to the degree that it releases him from lethargy, but ironic in that the search reveals its own counter principle. The difficulties Stencil encounters in getting beyond the words to a coherent picture of V. are a comment upon such quests; because the narrative omniscience of "Under the Rose" is dropped and replaced by the "forcible dislocations" of Stencil's personality, our attention is withdrawn from the scene beyond and focuses upon the narrative surface itself.

The Stencillized spectators in chapter three of *V.* overwhelm and obscure the actions they are witnessing for us. The reader, understandably, tears at the surface of these eight episodes, trying to patch together the continuity of spy story which he suspects exists below. In doing so, the reader engages himself in the very complexities Herbert Stencil faces as he tries to pierce the surface of third-hand information available to him. In the lexicon of *V.*'s last paragraph, we have only "surface phenomena" with which to discover what "lies beneath." Of course, the reader's concern for the submerged story misses the point; little of the spy drama bears any "plotted" relationship to the quest for V. (though each episode contributes to the diffusion of image and theme characteristic of Pynchon's writing). In fact, Stencil lifts from it only those references to a young girl named Victoria Wren, just as later he will read Fausto Maijstral's entire journal and fasten upon the references to his father, Sidney, and the Bad Priest, excluding the considerable and personal reflection in which they are embedded. The last of Stencil's impersonations is no more than a point of "vantage" (82). History is a point of view, a series of relations, in this example, to Herbert Stencil.

In Stencil's last appearance in the novel he "sketched the entire history of V. . . . and strengthened a long suspicion. That it did add up only to a recurrence of an initial and a few dead objects" (419). This same ugly thought occurs to Oedipa Maas, and we learn something about her motivation (and Pynchon's) by understanding Stencil's: "what love there was to Stencil had become directed entirely inward, toward the acquired sense of animateness. Having found this he could hardly release it, it was too dear. To sustain it he had to hunt V.; but if he should find her, where else would there be to go but back into half-consciousness? He tried not to think, therefore, about any end to the search. Approach and avoid" (44). Stencil's ambivalence is, like Oedipa's "ritual reluctance," a fear of self-destruction. His quest, nonetheless, is its own motive; it gives him life and separates him from the Inanimateness he finds, just as Oedipa's journey beyond her tower opens up the distance of consciousness between herself and the narcotized culture she discovers. For both, search is a way of surviving their own insights.

Many characters openly mock Stencil's pursuit, and the reader understands in the chapter "Valletta" that if Stencil has not found his "literal" V., he has found her meaning. When he continues to Stockholm, following the "frayed end of another clue" (425), we know that he cannot tolerate either the end of his chase or the symbolic significance which his literal pursuit has unveiled. Yet this is Pynchon's method: he takes us on a road which leads nowhere and has no terminus, but, like the taffy in Pirate Prentice's hell, "its labyrinthine path turns out, like Route One where it passes through the heart of Providence, to've been set up deliberately to give the stranger a tour of the city" (GR, 537). Stencil's hunt for scraps of V. will continue to enlarge her (or its) meaning, and though Oedipa never ascertains the existence of the Tristero, she does find the dark underside of her bright culture.

The pursuits of Stencil and Oedipa are examples, therefore, of the effort to find within the world the meaning of the world, to discover within time the true history outside of time. Pynchon develops this theme further in the story of Kurt Mondaugen, a young engineer stationed in Southwest Afrika. This character reappears in *Gravity's Rainbow* as a rocket engineer working under Weissmann. The setting for Mondaugen's recording of atmospheric radio disturbances is the brutal suppression of the Herero uprising in 1922, a nostalgic reminder for Herr Foppl of the decimation of the Hereros by von Trotha in 1904. Mondaugen is seeking among the "sferics" some pattern or message revealing their source, and his search for something intelligible from the "outside" serves as an oblique commentary on the macabre events of the world within Foppl's villa.

Near the end of the chapter Weissmann—who is another member of Foppl's siege party—bursts in on Mondaugen, claiming to have decoded one of the atmospheric "messages":

"It's your code. I've broken it. See: I remove every third letter and obtain: GODMEANTNUURK. This rearranged spells Kurt Mondaugen."

"Well, then," Mondaugen snarled. "And who the hell told you you could read my mail."

"The remainder of the message," Weissmann continued, "now reads: DIEWELTISTALLESWASDERFALLIST."

"The world is all that the case is," Mondaugen said. "I've heard that somewhere before." (258–59)

The line is the first proposition of Ludwig Wittgenstein's *Tractatus Logico-Philosophicus*, which first appeared in German in 1921. The *Tractatus* has an immediate relevance, for its theory of language addresses the relation of world and meaning which underlies Pynchon's fiction, as is apparent from Wittgenstein's preface:

Thus the aim of the book is to set a limit to thought, or rather—not to thought, but to the expression of thoughts: for in order to be able to set a limit to thought, we should have to find both sides of the limit thinkable (i.e. we should have to be able to think what cannot be thought).

It will therefore only be in language that the limit can be set, and what lies on the other side of the limit will simply be nonsense.[5]

Wittgenstein's opening proposition is an anti-message, telling us nothing about the world except that it is what it is. As such, the proposition conforms to Wittgenstein's announced intention of setting a limit to language, of concerning himself with what can be said, and is consistent with his insistence throughout the *Tractatus* that statements involving "value" or meaning in the world would have to be made from a position "outside" of the world. The relevance of the flat proposition, "The world is all that the case is," to the Herero chapter is precisely the cold recognition that our world includes such abominations as those exercised by von Trotha. By Wittgenstein's theory, whether or not those abominations have meaning, pattern, or sense to them lies beyond the power of language to declare: "The sense of the world must lie outside the world. In the world everything is as it is, and everything happens as it does happen. . . . For all that happens and is the case is accidental. . . . What makes it non-accidental cannot lie *within* the world, since if it did it would itself be accidental" (6.41).

Pynchon's appropriation of Wittgenstein, as in his use of Rilke and Weber, is double-edged, for Wittgenstein's theory serves to buttress in Pynchon's fiction the theme of mindless accident at the same time that it expresses the analytic consciousness of the "German mind" that is busy murdering Hereros with conscious design. The scope of the *Tractatus*, despite its own intentions, is philosophical, and argues only that events are "accidental" insofar as what we can "say" about them, not that history—could we know it—is in fact accidental. Pynchon's fiction perches exactly on that threshold, making a self-conscious use of metaphor ("a thrust at truth and a lie") to concern itself with both sides, the sense and the non-sense. His use of Wittgenstein, therefore, seems to rest upon Wittgenstein's keen awareness of language as a film between the two. His language theory does not gainsay for him or Pynchon the mysticism of existence ("*that* it exists," 6.44), only that what meaning there may be to it must lie outside of it; it is because of the precision of Wittgenstein's conditional that Pynchon finds in him a useful and apt thinker.

Mondaugen accuses Weissmann of "finagling" and the matter is never cleared up, but the anti-message from the "outside" has entered the story at the end of a nightmarish description of genocide. Pynchon has described for us what the case was; were these the workings of providence or accident?

Mircea Eliade and the Escape from History

The limit Wittgenstein poses is the limit we have been noting throughout Pynchon, for it is the linguistic version of the limit defined by our existence within the space-time continuum. Any meaning within requires a position without. Eliade's book *The Myth of the Eternal Return* discusses the role of man inside history and the various ways in which world religions have served the purpose of giving men a view of history outside of time which justifies such events as the Herero slaughters. Chapter four, "The Terror of History," defines what Eliade means by the problem of justifying historical events:

How justify, for example, the fact that southwestern Europe had to suffer for centuries—and hence renounce any impulse toward a higher historical existence, toward spiritual creation on the universal plane—for the sole reason that it happened to be on the road of the Asiatic invaders and later the neighbor of the Ottoman Empire? And in our day, when historical pressure no longer allows any escape, how can man tolerate the catastrophes and horrors of history—from collective deportations and massacres to atomic bombings—if beyond them he can glimpse no sign, no trans-historical meaning; if they are only the blind play of economic, social or political forces, or, even worse, only the result of the "liberties" a minority takes and exercises directly on the stage of universal history?[6]

Eliade's either/or construction parallels those of Pynchon and demonstrates the ambiguity inherent in explanations of history. His book focuses upon the ways in which "archaic" man dealt with the terror of uncertainty. Archaic man reduced historical events to archetypal "repetitions" as a way of participating in a timelessness outside of time, in a mythic eternal present, and thereby eliminating all sense of a linear succession of discrete and irreversible events. Eliade argues that a linear model of history has replaced the concept of "eternal return" and that this linear model is less effective than the cyclical idea, for it requires a "redemption" of historical events at the end of history, as is true of Christian eschatology.

The Zone-Hereros are Pynchon's example of a people caught with a foot in either camp: one cyclical and returning, the other western and Christian, linear and "one-way." Eliade's account of the history of the myth of eternal return is widely respected, and such discussions of that myth are clearly one source of Pynchon's use of such words as "return," "Center," "history," "faith," and "irreversible" in the story of the Zone-Hereros. While these words have a wide applicability throughout Pynchon's writings, they cluster in *Gravity's Rainbow* around the hopes of the displaced Herero, Oberst Enzian. Eliade's analysis helps explain Enzian's motivation, which springs from the Herero tribal history.

In the chapter which provides most of Enzian's background (314–29) we are told that he was corrupted by the events of history long before he met Weissmann in Africa. In 1904 60 percent of the Herero population was exterminated by the "blue devils" from the North, the Germans under General von Trotha.

The rest were being used like animals. Enzian grew up into a white-occupied world. Captivity, sudden death, one-way departures were the ordinary things of every day. By the time the question occurred to him, he could find no way to account for his own survival. He could not believe in any process of selection. Ndjambi Karunga and the Christian God were too far away. There was no difference between the behavior of a god and the operations of pure chance. (323)

In the pages which follow Enzian also reveals that he has put himself at some distance from his initial awe of the Rocket and Germany's civilization after Weissmann brought him back from Africa. He has grown cold, less naive (324). Later, talking with Slothrop in Berlin, Enzian remarks, "To those of us who survived von Trotha, it also means that we have learned to stand outside our history and watch it, without feeling too much. . . . A sense for the statistics of our being" (362).

That statistical sensibility is closely allied with the narrative view present in the entire work of Pynchon, for statistics are an interface between the discrete operations or events of chance and the patterns which inhere in events in the mass. Given this awareness, Enzian's preoccupation with the second rocket in the series (00001) is somewhat puzzling, but Enzian's intentions are a species of the cyclical return Eliade describes, as the narrator explains: "What Enzian wants to create will have no history. It will never need a design change. Time, as time is known to the

other nations, will wither away inside this new one. The Erd-
schweinhöhle will not be bound, like the Rocket, to time. The
people will find the Center again, the Center without time, the
journey without hysteresis, where every departure is a return to
the same place, the only place . . ." (318–19).[7]

Enzian's hope for a return to Center is paralleled by the inverse
and nihilistic intentions of a competing Herero leader, Josef Ombindi. Ombindi, too, seeks to control history, but his method is
tribal suicide, which he sells as seeking the "Final Zero." Ombindi heads the forces within the Schwarzkommando "who have
opted for sterility and death. The struggle is mostly in silence . . .
but it is political struggle. No one is more troubled with it than
Enzian" (316). Enzian is not of those forces; to believe so is to
misunderstand the motivation behind the Schwarzkommando's
search for the Rocket and one of the book's major subplots. Any
interpretation of the Zone-Hereros must recognize this dualism
within the ranks, and see that their parallel structural hope
(Zero/Center) masks opposing intentions.

A section of Eliade's book, "The Symbolism of the Center,"
helps gloss what Enzian has in mind. Eliade explains that the
Center was considered the meeting place of heaven, earth, and
hell; it was an axis mundi. The Center is also "the point at which
the Creation began," embodying the universe in its essence. The
Center "is pre-eminently the zone of the sacred, the zone of absolute reality. Similarly, all the other symbols of absolute reality
(trees of life and immortality, Fountain of Youth, etc.) are also
situated at the Center."[8]

This absolute reality at the Center is what Enzian seeks. The
religious system and cosmology of the Herero tribe are an instance of the pattern Eliade describes; his analysis is confirmed by
the anthropology of H. G. Luttig's *The Religious System and
Social Organization of the Herero*, which links Eliade's definition
of the Center with the Herero version and gives further evidence
of Pynchon's care in such matters of fact:

When mention is made among the Herero of the "land over the sea" or
the "region in the north," reference is made to the underworld. It is to
this abode that the dead depart, for they are buried facing that region. The
cattle sacrificed to the ancestors are killed in such a position that their
heads also face that direction. The netherworld is not only the abode of

the dead and the place of annihilation, but it is also a place where new life is created. This fact, which is common to most other primitive religions, is apparent from the conception of the rebirth of the sun in the netherworld. This region can therefore be conceived as the locality whence the Herero tribe came. There is situated the mythical tree of life, from which the first ancestral pair, Mukuru with his wife Kamangarunga, and their cattle, sprang.[9]

Pynchon's description of the Herero mythology (315–33 especially) is accurate in every respect, including his peculiar account of "the woman alone in the earth, planted up to her shoulders in the aardvark hole" (315). This account is part of Luttig's discussion of the Ovatjimba (the clan to which Pynchon refers) and their totem animal, the "ant-bear": "The second report gives a better illustration of the supernatural character of the ant-bear. It mentions a myth which relates of a woman all of whose children were stillborn, and who was cured after having been placed in the ant-bear hole."[10] Luttig's book also includes a diagram of the Herero village structure in the shape of a mandala and discusses how that structure was for the tribe an image of their cosmology.

Enzian and the other Zone-Hereros are a corrupted version of the tribal system Luttig describes. Their "archaic" mythology no longer has absolute claim on them, and Enzian is full of doubt:

But we, Zone-Hereros, under the earth, how long will we wait in this north, this locus of death? Is it to be reborn? or have we really been buried for the last time, buried facing north like all the rest of our dead, and like all the holy cattle ever sacrificed to the ancestors? . . . The history of the old Hereros is one of lost messages. It began in mythical times, when the sly hare who nests in the Moon brought death among men, instead of the Moon's true message. The true message has never come. Perhaps the Rocket is meant to take us there someday, and then the Moon will tell us its truth at last. (322)

Enzian's enterprise, though full of doubt, is not an act of self-destruction but one seeking value in the repetition of the archetypal First Firing in which Weissmann sent Gottfried aloft. This is what he has in mind, and why even near the end of the book the Schwarzkommando are still trying to find the exact location of Weissmann's firing (Pynchon, for obvious reasons, chose the actual locale of the Luneburg Heath, which could not fail to have increased meaning for the Hereros), and to discover what was special about that rocket. They finally obtain these facts from Thanatz, though the narrator keeps them from the reader. Because the repetition of the First Firing entails Enzian's own death, the factions within the ranks ("Empty, Neutral and Green") are unified for the first time "since the dividing along lines of racial life and racial death began, how many years ago, reconciled for now in the only Event that could have brought them together" (673).

The firing of the Rocket into true North has an archetypal significance for the displaced Hereros which it did not have for Weissmann and Gottfried. But for the Hereros, true North is their absolute center, where there is no time, where departure and return, like the cycle of the sun, are the same thing. Enzian's rocket will fly both to the North and to the moon, since (as Luttig explains) the two locales are merged in the Herero belief: "we are now in a position to conclude that the power in the moon is the same as that of the netherworld. Here again the ambivalent character of the underworld is evident. The power of this region both causes and punishes evil. As an illustration of this we repeat that the hare belongs to this region having his abode in the moon and in spite of which he is punished for his deception."[11] Enzian himself understands: "There are those down in the Erdschwein-höhle, younger ones who've only known white autumn-prone Europe, who believe Moon is their destiny. But older ones can remember that Moon, like Ndjambi Karunga, is both the bringer of evil and its avenger" (322).

Thus the Second Firing will be more than a repetition of the First, in which Gottfried's double will be carried North; it will be, the Hereros think, a Return to the North, the underworld, and the moon, where the original message will be redeemed and the Hereros taken out of time. The folly of their effort is self-evident, for it is hybrid, as they themselves are a hybrid people: the Zone-Hereros, who know only second-hand their former tribal customs and who have been infected with the disease of Christianity (320–21). The Second Firing will be at once a tragic mimicry of Weissmann's "one-way" European despair and a mockery of their former cyclical cosmology.

Enzian has reservations about the Event, and this mitigates his action; the narrator's view is apparent from his ironic allusion to

Marx's famous prediction: "Time, as time is known to the other nations, will wither away inside this new one" (319). Nevertheless, Enzian represents one of Pynchon's most poignant examples of those characters who pursue their destinies despite the doubts which persecute them.

I. P. Pavlov and "operational paranoia"

Enzian and the Hereros attempt to escape time altogether; for them the providential ordering of the Christian god, or of Ndjambi Karunga, has become indistinguishable from the orders which inhere in the laws of chance. For most of the other characters in *Gravity's Rainbow*, a belief in conspiracy directed at them is preferable to a Situation lacking any coherence; for them paranoia is a source of communion and order establishing reason behind the "terror of history." Moreover, the paranoia of these characters is not fully psychotic, for their vision of conspiracies is an "operational paranoia" which discovers connections that have an actual basis in economic and political reality.[12] The most far-reaching of these discoveries echoes Sidney Stencil's recognition that "any Situation takes shape from events much lower than the merely human" (*V.*, 455), and uses paranoia to insist upon a chemical continuity within which human life is only a bright arc in the chemistry of time and space.

Paranoia satisfies Eliade's only criterion for evaluating the effectiveness of historical models: its extreme rationality discerns purpose and coherence operating behind the appearance of chance. What that purpose may be and who might lie behind it remain unclear, however, making paranoia a very anxious and precarious defense. Thomas Gwenhidwy, one of the psychologists working at St. Veronica's hospital, propounds a paranoid version of history to Edward Pointsman. Gwenhidwy's theory arises from his fear of the V-2 rockets landing on London. All the characters in *Gravity's Rainbow*'s first section are afraid of the rockets; for some, their fear mushrooms into a persecution complex. Gwenhidwy's suspicions of why the rockets are striking the East End instead of Whitehall have all the signs of paranoia, yet they prompt a view of history which possesses the determinism Eliade describes in the passage cited above (p. 83):

"In some cities the rich live upon the heights, and the poor are found below. In others the rich occupy the shoreline, while the poor must live inland. Now in London, here is a gra-dient of wretchedness? increasing as the river widens to the sea. I am only ask-ing, why? Is it because of the shipping? Is it in the pat-terns of land use, especially those relating to the Industrial Age? Is it a case of an-cient tribal tabu, surviving down all the Eng-lish generations? No. The true reason is the Threat From the East, you see. And the South: from the mass of Europe, certainly. The people out here were *meant to go down first.* . . . But what if the Ci-ty were a growing neo-plasm, across the centuries, always changing, to meet exactly the chang-ing shape of its very worst, se-cret fears? . . ."

"You're right, Gwenhidwy," judicious, sipping his tea, "that is very paranoid." (172–73)

Any number of characters can be cited: Tyrone "has become ob-sessed with the idea of a rocket with his name written on it" (25); Tchitcherine, Enzian's half-brother and Soviet secret agent, seeks the reason behind his assignment to the wastes of Central Asia, and "in his moments of sickest grandeur it is quite clear to him how his own namesake and the murdered Jew Rathenau put to-gether an elaborate piece of theatre at Rapallo, and that the real and only purpose was to reveal to Vaslav Tchitcherine the exis-tence of Enzian" (352); and Horst Achtfaden, a V-2 engineer cap-tured by the Schwarzkommando, views the critical events of 1904 as a series whose motive has been his present incarceration (452). All these characters rationalize history as a conspiracy directed against themselves.

Such rationalizaton of history is presented in *Gravity's Rain-bow* as the persistence of a Puritan frame of mind, a derivation Pynchon establishes in the growing suspicions of Slothrop fol-lowing his battle with Grigori the octopus: "it's a Puritan reflex of seeking other orders behind the visible, also known as paranoia" (188). Paranoid order becomes in *Gravity's Rainbow* the modern equivalent of the Puritan's providence; this is implied in the nar-rator's diction, which is drawn from the definition of "sacra-ment" in *The Book of Common Prayer*: "an outward and visible sign of inward and spiritual grace." As noted earlier, Pynchon's use of the Puritan vocabulary is allied with Weber's analysis in *The Protestant Ethic and the Spirit of Capitalism*. Weber's well-known book discusses the Calvinist strain of Protestantism as a rational religion, and demonstrates the relationship between the believer's fear of not being a member of the predetermined elect and the drive to establish material success as an outward sign of inward grace. His book is the proper source for a full understanding of Pynchon's use of such words as "grace," "invisible," "Elect," and God's "hand" or "finger."

Pynchon links paranoia to the Puritan frame of mind not only to invoke Weber's sociological analysis but also to suggest the origins of that paranoia in the rational heritage of western civilization. Paranoia itself, according to Hendrik Hertzberg and David McClelland, is a "recent cultural disorder" which "follows the adoption of rationalism as the quasi-official religion of Western man. . . . Paranoia substitutes a rigorous (though false) order for chaos, and at the same time dispels the sense of individual insignificance by making the paranoid the focus of all he sees going on around him—a natural response to the confusion of modern life."[13]

Much has been written about the relationship of Puritanism and paranoia in Pynchon's writings,[14] but that rational spiritualism is balanced in *Gravity's Rainbow* by I. P. Pavlov's physiological explanation of paranoia. Pavlov's physiological explanation assumes that matter precedes mind; the subject's mental disorder results from a pathology of thinking tissue and is not any consequence of what the subject thinks. Pavlov's explanation represents in the domain of psychology a thoroughly cause-and-effect world-view, a mechanical materialism opposed to the "psychological" interpretations of paranoia put forth by his contemporary Pierre Janet.

Pavlov's discussion of paranoia was published in chapter XIV of *Conditioned Reflexes and Psychiatry*, translated into English by Horsley Gantt (1941). This is "The Book" Edward Pointsman treasures. Pavlov's thought dictates Pointsman's thinking, and is used by Pynchon as one pole of the ambiguous presentation of paranoia in *Gravity's Rainbow*. The novel is thick with behavioral terminology, and that theory of behavior is part of the book's threatening determinism, in which history is a large Skinner box and "freedom" is an illusion of our conditioning. Slothrop's search for "other orders behind the visible" is described as both "Puritan" and a "reflex." The two together, "Puritan reflex," form another expression of that dissonance throughout Pynchon between a purely mechanical view of life's activity and the suggestion of another "order" transcending cause-and-effect history. In *Gravity's Rainbow* paranoia is the vehicle to that other possibility, and Pointsman's insistence on the physiological basis of paranoia establishes the profane extreme to which the spiritual possibility is tied.

Pointsman hopes to prove Pavlov's mechanical explanation and win the Nobel Prize. This is the source of his powerful interest in Slothrop, whom he believes to be a classical example of a "psychopathically deviant, obsessive, . . . latent paranoiac" (90). The reason for his belief is that Tyrone's map of stars, which records his love affairs, accords exactly with Roger Mexico's map of rocket strikes, noted by circles. Tyrone's affairs always precede the rocket blasts, however, and in this mysterious reversal of cause and effect (since, Pointsman reasons, the rockets must have some role as "stimulus" in Slothrop's sex life) Pointsman sees a perfect embodiment of Pavlov's explanation of the *sentiments d'emprise* (translated: "Feelings in the Delusions of Persecution"). To his trained eye, this seeming reversal of stimulus and response represents a confusion of the "idea of the opposite," a concept Pointsman read about in chapter LIV of Gantt's translation, which is Pavlov's response to Pierre Janet's psychological explanation of paranoia:

Our general idea of the opposite is a fundamental and indispensable idea which, combined with other general ideas, facilitates, disposes and, even, alone makes possible our normal thought. My relations with the surrounding world, including the social milieu, as well as my attitude face to face with myself, necessarily undergoes serious injury if I constantly confuse contrary ideas or situations; myself and not myself, mine and yours, I am at the same time alone and in society, I offend and I am offended, etc. Consequently it is necessary to have a reason, if there is abolition or weakening of this general idea; and this reason, one can and one must look for, to my mind, in the fundamental laws of nervous activity.[15]

Pavlov felt that the idea of the opposite was weakened in three "transmarginal" phases: "equalization," "paradoxical," and "ultraparadoxical." In "equalization" the strength of the stimulus ceases to matter; in the "paradoxical" phase the subject responds not to a strong stimulus but a weak one; and in the "ultrapara-doxical" the subject responds to a negative or inhibitory stimulus.[16] Pavlov felt that the "ultraparadoxical" phase was the condition in which subjects lost their ability to distinguish opposites.

This is the theory which informs the conversation between Pointsman and Spectro on pages 48 and 49 of *Gravity's Rainbow*. Pavlovian "stimulus and response" is a species of the more general "cause and effect":

The true mechanical explanation always remains the ideal of natural sciences; the knowledge of reality, including that of ourselves, one can only approach slowly, and over a long period. The whole of the exact sciences of today make only a long chain of progressive approximations of mechanical interpretation, approximations all of the steps of which are united by the supreme principle of determinism: no effect without cause.[17]

Pointsman's explanation of Pavlov's view to Roger Mexico (88–89) follows the words of his master almost verbatim. Like Pavlov, Pointsman is opposed to the complementarity of Janet's mystical psychology: "'Pierre Janet—sometimes the man talked like an Oriental mystic. He had no real grasp of the opposites. "The act of injuring and the act of being injured are joined in the behavior of the whole injury." . . . The last refuge of the incorrigibly lazy, Mexico, is just this sort of yang-yin rubbish. One avoids all manner of unpleasant lab work that way, but what has one *said?*'" (88). Janet's theories are part of that enterprise in *Gravity's Rainbow* representing the forces of inseparability. Roland Feldspath, Leni Pokler, Fahringer's Zen rocketry,[18] and Mexico's "angel's-eye view" all undermine Pointsman's mechanical view. Pointsman can't accept what Mexico tells him: "Bombs are not dogs. No link. No memory. No conditioning"; this statistical approach "wrecks the elegant rooms of history, threatens the idea of cause and effect itself" (56).

The entire weight of *Gravity's Rainbow* calls the absoluteness of that idea into question, and moves both characters and readers into the uncertain ground between the distinctness of successive events and the timeless complementarities of meaning. Pointsman himself is subject to that manipulation. In his effort to defend Pavlov and show his master's ideas at work in Slothrop's behavior, Pointsman finds himself enunciating a viewpoint which is akin to the possibility that *Gravity's Rainbow* suggests:

Spectro shakes his head. "You're putting response before stimulus."

"Not at all. Think of it. He's out there, and he can *feel them coming,* days in advance. But it's a reflex. A reflex to something that's in the air *right now.* Something we're too coarsely put together to sense—but *Slothrop can.*" (49)

Unwittingly, Pointsman is suggesting the omnipresent reality implied by the book as a whole. His notion that Tyrone might be responding to a future event that is present *"now"* subverts cause and effect, which relies upon the succession in time of causes before effects. His effort to create a plausible defense for his position heightens instead the possibility that stimulus and response are inseparable parts of one process, and that Tyrone feels the rockets coming just as the narrator can feel the rocket's arrival on the last page of the book. For within the four-dimensional narrative vision, the rocket has already arrived, its point of impact coincidental with Blicero's cry in "The Clearing," "Räumen."

Pynchon's ironic use of Pavlov's terminology against Pointsman persists as he moves through "transmarginal phases." One night Pointsman is awakened, not by the roaring squadrons overhead but by "Gwenhidwy's small, reluctant tap. . . . Something like what happens on the cortex of Dog during the 'paradoxical' phase" (138). Gwenhidwy has come to tell him that Kevin Spectro, another owner of "The Book," has been killed in a rocket blast, the fifth of the owners to die. Pointsman begins to suspect a pattern, and his paranoid ruminations oscillate between fear and delusions of grandeur, as he "feels patterns on his cortex going dark" (141), which is Pavlov's description of the neuron activity in animals moving through transmarginal phases. Pointsman drifts briefly into the ultraparadoxical phase when he suspects (correctly) that his own plot against Slothrop is only part of a much larger one, and that he is "a control that is out of control." The idea of the opposite is almost displaced in Pointsman's consciousness by Janet's complementarity: "'Yang and Yin,' whispers the Voice, 'Yang and Yin . . .'" (277–78). Pointsman manages to fend off that view and is dismissed at last by the narrator: "he'll be left only with Cause and Effect, and the rest of his sterile armamentarium" (752).

Pointsman's desire to demonstrate the physiological basis of paranoia in Slothrop is frustrated by the mix-up at Putzi's that results in Major Marvey's castration. But the paranoia which Slothrop, Gwenhidwy, and other characters in *Gravity's Rainbow* exhibit is justified in large measure by the economic and political orders unveiled by the book. This element of their "operational paranoia" (25) is one of the least ambiguous aspects of *Gravity's Rainbow*, for the order "behind the appearance of diversity and enterprise" (165) is never questioned by the book and is affirmed in our own world beyond it. As Slothrop says to Tantivy: "'Paranoia's ass. Something's up, a-and you know it!'" (192). Tyrone has actually been the object of a "Father Conspiracy"; he is the object of a plot constructed by Pointsman, and Pointsman's plot is itself entangled in the webs of machinations still higher. About this there is no uncertainty.

The economic basis of historical events revealed in the paranoid mode of the book becomes another level of history under the rose, and underlies the transvaluation of war that is a persistent theme of the narrator: "Don't forget the real business of the War is buying and selling. . . . The true war is a celebration of markets. Organic markets, carefully styled 'black' by the professionals, spring up everywhere" (105). That paranoid tone has a predecessor in Randolph Bourne, who wrote of the war effort in 1917, "We are learning that war doesn't need enthusiasm, doesn't need conviction, doesn't need hope, to sustain it. Once manoeuvered, it takes care of itself, provided only that our industrial rulers see that the end of the war will leave American capital in a strategic position for world-enterprise."[19]

The "industrial rulers" of the "professional" white market are opposed to the "organic markets, carefully styled 'black.'" The outlines of this economic battle appear early in the book as one vein of meaning embedded in Feldspath's cryptic remarks: "All these things arise from one difficulty: control. For the first time it was *inside*, do you see. . . . A market needed no longer to be run by the Invisible Hand, but now could *create itself*—its own logic, momentum, style, from *inside*" (30). The White market / Black market dualism is a species of the Inside/Outside structure permeating Pynchon's writing, and parallels the Conradian North/South colonial themes, the racial commentary implicit in the colors (and in Pynchon's use of King Kong and Malcolm X), the white toilet / black shit motif, and the controlling antiphony of form and chance. Here the white market is opposed to the randomness of Adam Smith's economic theory of the "Invisible Hand" and prefers the rational predictability of a system without unknowns.

This economic polarity doesn't reduce to a struggle between good and evil, for in this "organic" market everything is "negotiable"—including Jews, "every bit as negotiable as cigarettes, cunt, or Hershey bars" (105). When Slothrop meets Geli Tripping, he doesn't ask her where she got the Baby Ruth candy bar "because he knows" (291). The black, organic, market, however, possesses the virtues of being local, taking place among individuals, and satisfying specific, immediate human needs. Readers are enlivened by the "black" episodes in *Gravity's Rainbow*: when Schnorp and Slothrop escape "Marvy's Mothers"; when Mexico pisses on the corporate gathering; and when Mexico and Bodine disrupt the Utgarthaloki dinner party. If anything in the book cheers, it is the impulse toward disruption and spontaneity which typifies the "ad hoc adventure" (706). Their success is short-lived but communal; the gross alliterations of Bodine and Mexico gain adherents at the party, as some of the guests show their true "gaudy" colors by joining in. The butler holding the door for them as they leave is an example: " 'Pimple pie with filth frosting, gentlemen,' he nods. And just at the other side of dawning, you can see a smile" (717). The butler, of course, is black.

At the Pig-Hero festival a black market springs up in the village streets and "weeds of paranoia begin to bloom" in Slothrop's mind, not because he fears the black market itself but because he knows what it will bring down upon them all:

Materializing from their own weird office silence, the coppers show up now, two black 'n' white charabancs full of bluegreen uniforms, white armbands, little bucket hats with starburst insignia, truncheons already unsheathed, black dildos in nervous hands, wobbling, ready for action. . . . The War must've been lean times for crowd control, murder and mopery was the best you could do, one suspect at a time. But now, with the White Market to be protected, here again are whole streets full of bodies eager for that erste Abreibung, and you can bet the heat are happy with it. (569–70)

The international implications of the White Market's ambitions are revealed in a dialogue between Tchitcherine and Wimpe, a chemicals salesman who possesses "a streak of unhealthy enthusiasm . . . for organic chemistry" (344). Wimpe explains to Vaslav an effort underway which is global in scope, "to find something that can kill intense pain without causing addiction." Wimpe's description of the results of this search ties the conversation to the inherent ambiguity of the Situation Pynchon's fiction outlines: "'Results have not been encouraging. We seem up against a dilemma built into Nature, much like the Heisenberg situation. There is nearly complete parallelism between analgesia and addiction. The more pain it takes away, the more we desire it. It appears we can't have one property without the other, any more than a particle physicist can specify position without suffering an uncertainty as to the particle's velocity—'" (348). Wimpe and the people for whom he works want to abolish addiction because it is a false need over which they have no control. It has nothing to do with real pain and is therefore an unknown factor in the economy. To the degree that Pig Bodine and Säure Bummer disturb that economy, their dope addictions are salutary. Wimpe's people want a predictable market: "A rational economy cannot depend on psychological quirks. We could not plan . . ." (348–49).

Tchitcherine cannot believe that Wimpe is trafficking in pain, but his belief in a world of competing nation-states is as outmoded as the Machiavellian politics of Sidney Stencil. The "chemical cartel is the model for the very structure of nations," Wimpe informs him (349). But it is only later, under a burgeoning paranoia, that Tchitcherine grasps the truth: "Oh, Wimpe. Old V-Mann, were you right? Is your IG to be *the very model of nations?*" (566).[20]

Tchitcherine's paranoid certainty is an economic version of the tremendous connectedness exhibited by the text of *Gravity's Rainbow*, an awareness characterized by the narrator as "the discovery that *everything is connected*, everything in the Creation" (703). The revolutionary aspect of the paranoid awareness is the sense of connectedness paranoia induces. By contrast, official history works to keep events separate, like distinct particles on a one-way timeline. Jessica takes Roger away from this "sterile history—a known past, a projectable future. . . . Suddenly there was a beach, the unpredictable" (126).

Such connectedness is not salvation, for Roger hoped that through Jessica "everything could be changed and she could always deny the dark sea at his back, love it away" (126), and this is not a hope which *Gravity's Rainbow* fulfills. But the book does affirm the simultaneous worlds and histories which official history has denied or overlooked; this kind of pluralism underlies the "unspoken agreement about not stomping on bugs in Säure's place" (621) and the marvelous simultaneity of the Christmas bugs' world embedded in the straw of Christ's manger (173–74). The most intricate and far-reaching of the book's affirmations insists on the continuity between mineral and human life, for as Sidney Stencil knew, "any Situation takes shape from events much lower than the merely human" (*V.*, 455). Stencil's sober knowledge reappears in *Gravity's Rainbow* through the delusions of grandeur of Nora Dodson-Truck: "In recent weeks, in true messianic style, it has come clear to her that her real identity is, literally, the Force of Gravity. *I am Gravity, I am That against which the Rocket must struggle, to which the prehistoric wastes submit and are transmuted to the very substance of History . . .*" (639). Nora's paranoia recognizes the largest context in which human affairs take place, and reminds us that human history is but an "outward-and-visible fraction" (612) of the chemical process of the universe.

Chemistry is the basis of the molecular pluralism in *Gravity's Rainbow*. In the world of molecules distinctions between animal and mineral life disappear, just as the distinction between "life" and "death" is lost in the process of transmutation that joins them. That chemical reality is given voice in *Gravity's Rainbow* and serves to undermine the human effort to falsify the chemical process in the creation of a plastic reality.

The book early declares its chemical vision in what may be a parody of Wordsworth's "Composition upon Westminster Bridge": "The sun is still below the horizon. The day feels like rain, but for now the air is uncommonly clear. The great power station, and the gasworks beyond, stand precisely: crystals grown in the morning's beaker, stacks, vents, towers, plumbing, gnarled emissions of steam and smoke . . ." (6).[21] History is chemistry here; the City itself, archetype of civilization, is a crystal in the beaker of time. Pynchon ties that chemical metaphor to economics, for it is "out of that global stratum, most deeply laid," that "all appearances of corporate ownership really spring" (243).

The continuity of the mineral world "below" and the corporate economics of the white world "above" is the most important expression in Pynchon of the relations between depth and surface, and of the idea of life as a bright arc which has its beginning and end in the chemical realignments of the world below. The social expression of that continuity is established in The Crying of Lot 49 by the congruence of Tristero with the "cheered land"; in Gravity's Rainbow the path of the Rocket integrates the rainbow arc "that we are allowed to see" with "the other silent world" (726). This chemical continuity is the vision Walter Rathenau tries to convey to the Nazis, using words which recall the opening pages of Gravity's Rainbow: "You are off on a winding and difficult road, which you conceive to be wide and straight. . . . Is it any use for me to tell you that all you believe is illusion?" Rathenau directs them to the coal-tars deep in the earth, for their Reich, he says, is not "resurrection" but only the polymerization of "a few dead molecules." The Nazis' belief in their Reich is part of the narrow view of history which the book undermines: "All talk of cause and effect is secular history, and secular history is a diversionary tactic. . . . If you want the truth . . . you must look into . . . the hearts of certain molecules—it is they after all which dictate temperatures, pressures, rates of flow, costs, profits, the shapes of towers . . ." (167).

Rathenau's words attribute a consciousness to the molecular world. Later, in Central Asia, the character Blobadjian is "taken" below into that molecular world, where he learns from a committee on molecular structure "how alphabetic is the nature of molecules": "These are our letters, our words: they too can be modulated, broken, recoupled, redefined, co-polymerized one to the other in worldwide chains that will surface now and then over long molecular silences, like the seen parts of a tapestry" (355).

That succinct description of the chemical process—"broken, recoupled, redefined, co-polymerized"—is used by Pynchon as a metaphor operating not only in the syntheses of nature but in the artificial duplication of that process by man. Slothrop's train to Zurich imitates "industrial synthesis" as its cars are "broken up, put together, coupled and recoupled" (257); Enzian's amphetamine-induced paranoia suggests that the bombing of the Jamf-Olfabriken Werke AG is really "the exact industrial process of conversion . . . coding, recoding, redecoding the holy Text" (520–21); and the metaphor appears in Webley Silvernail's "guest performance" (before the rats), a performance which recalls Eliade's suspicion that history may be determined by an "elite few": "Now it's back to the cages and the rationalized forms of death—death in the service of the one species cursed with the knowledge that it will die. . . . 'I would set you free, if I knew how. But it isn't free out here. All the animals, plants, the minerals, even other kinds of men, are being broken and reassembled every day, to preserve an elite few, who are the loudest to theorize on freedom, but the least free of all'" (230). As Webley's eloquence implies, the chemistry of the universe has been abstracted and used against the world from which it came.

This fact accounts for the significance of the Imipolex G which Tyrone seeks, and which surrounds Gottfried in the Rocket 00000; Imipolex G is "an aromatic heterocyclic polymer," one of the products of "Plasticity's central canon: that chemists were no longer to be at the mercy of Nature. They could decide now what properties they wanted a molecule to have, and then go ahead and build it" (249). This opposition between Plastic and Nature is traced to the corruption of Kekulé's dream, placed in the marvelous Pokler section at the heart of Gravity's Rainbow. The movement this passage outlines from organic to inorganic should be seen as a "routinization" of Nature's processes, and the same series—animal, plant, mineral—used in Webley Silvernail's speech appears again here:

But the meanness, the cynicism with which this dream is to be used. The Serpent that announces, "The world is a closed thing, cyclical, resonant, eternally-returning," is to be delivered into a system whose only aim is to violate the Cycle. Taking and not giving back, demanding that "productivity" and "earnings" keep on increasing with time, the System removing from the rest of the World these vast quantities of energy to keep its own tiny desperate fraction showing a profit: and not only most of humanity—most of the World, animal, vegetable and mineral, is laid waste in the process." (412)

The cycle which the Serpent announces includes death; the System, in its futile effort to elude this fate, creates "rationalized forms of death" which use tremendous energy and lay waste the world.

The Rocket is Pynchon's symbol of all this. The history of the V-2 documents the subservience of man to machine and illustrates the voracious appetite of the rocket as it used potatoes for fuel, starving its own people to kill the Dutch and English. Moreover, the Rocket is not only Pynchon's symbol of technology, for by its very nature the V-2 participates in the larger vision of chemical continuity that leaches through *Gravity's Rainbow*. The Rocket, as "an entire system *won*, away from the feminine darkness, held against the entropies of lovable but scatterbrained Mother Nature" (324), must "sooner or later fall" (747).

Gravity dominates everywhere: *"there is always the danger of falling"* (723). Gravity, like the Herero's Ndjambi Karunga, both destroys and renews. The process of natural synthesis, as described by Victor Weisskopf of M.I.T., occurs under the pressure of gravity:

The gravitational force goes on pulling the atoms together, so that the cluster becomes smaller and denser. The atoms "fall" toward the center under the pull of gravity. During this fall they acquire speed; when they get into dense regions, they will collide with other atoms and transmit the energy of their motion to the rest of the material. So the contraction of the cluster causes the atoms to move faster and faster and collide with each other. Gravitational energy is transformed into irregular heat motion.[22]

Pynchon knows this; his books have always been about the transmutation of "waste" as the message system of the universe. This universal process goes well beyond human understanding, but the process itself is one that Pynchon presents through the experiences of characters on the Other Side. Weisskopf's calm explanation surfaces as the magical wonder of Lyle Bland's discovery "that Gravity, taken so for granted, is really something eerie . . . having hugged to its holy center the wastes of dead species, gathered, packed, transmuted, realigned, and rewoven molecules" (590).

This is not much consolation to those who demand "salvation" outside of time, for the timelessness Pynchon invokes exists at once with the time that man seeks to transcend. *Gravity's Rainbow* is the drama of that complex determinism, and cautions that the danger of our freedom lies not in the certainty of falling but in the vertical solutions we erect against that knowledge. This is Silvernail's message to the rats. While there is no indication in the book that death can be defeated, the chemical world of *Gravity's Rainbow* does open up a "beyond" which reminds us that what we call "life" and "death" is but a fraction of a process much larger, and that the systems created by the fear of death are destroying even the narrow, colorful band of that process we experience as life.

NOTES

1. (New York: New American Library, 1968), pp. 1178–79. The quotation which introduces this chapter is also from this edition, p. 986.
2. *The Education of Henry Adams* (New York: Modern Library, 1931), p. 495.
3. *The Noble Savage*, no. 3 (1961), 223–51.
4. *Ibid.*, pp. 227–28, 248–49.
5. Trans. D. F. Pears and B. F. McGuinness (London: Routledge & Kegan Paul, 1961), p. 3. It must be cautioned that Wittgenstein's *Tractatus* is a theory of language, not the world, and one which he altered considerably under the criticism of Frank Ramsey. Wittgenstein's ideas at the time were heavily influenced by his engineering background; his view of language was an ideal view of a logical language isomorphic with thought and the world. This identity is not even perfectly stated in the *Tractatus*, which is self-contradictory, and is amended in the less systematic writings of his later years, especially *The Philosophical Investigations*. See A. J. Ayer's *Language, Truth and Logic* and G. E. M. Anscombe's *An Introduction to Wittgenstein's Tractatus*. William Plater's "imaginative" equating of the "closed system" with Wittgenstein's theory of language seems to me a misunderstanding of both Wittgenstein and Pynchon. See Plater, *Grim Phoenix*, p. 244, n. 4.
6. Trans. Willard R. Trask (London: Routledge & Kegan Paul, 1955), p. 151.

7. "Hysteresis" is a word originally meaning "to be behind, to lag," and is used in physics to refer to a "retardation of the effect."

8. Eliade, *Myth*, pp. 16–18.

9. (Utrecht, 1933), p. 13.

10. *Ibid.*, p. 53.

11. *Ibid.*, pp. 15–16.

12. Cf. Mendelson's view of the paranoia of *Gravity's Rainbow* as a "distorting lens" which the reader corrects, yielding a "plausible" vision of the world ("Gravity's Encyclopedia," p. 181).

13. "Paranoia," *Harper's Magazine*, 248 (June, 1974), 51–54. This article is particularly intriguing because the authors use *The Crying of Lot 49* as part of their discussion.

14. See, for example, Siegel's *Creative Paranoia*, and Scott Sanders, "Pynchon's Paranoid History," in *Mindful Pleasures*, ed. Levine and Leverenz, pp. 139–59.

15. I. P. Pavlov, "Les Sentiments D'Emprise and the Ultraparadoxical Phase," in *Conditioned Reflexes and Psychiatry*, trans. Horsley Gantt (New York: International Publisher Co., 1941), p. 147.

16. See Pavlov's *Conditioned Reflexes: An Investigation of the Physiological Activity of the Cerebral Cortex*, trans. G. V. Anrep (New York: Oxford University Press, 1927), pp. 271–76.

17. Pavlov, *Conditioned Reflexes and Psychiatry*, p. 149.

18. Fahringer's view of the Rocket as arrow (403) is an allusion to Eugen Herrigel's *Zen in the Art of Archery*, trans. R. F. C. Hull (New York: Vintage Books, 1953).

19. *War and the Intellectuals*, ed. and intro. by Carl Resek (New York: Harper Torchbooks, 1964), p. 39.

20. The truth of this is to be found in the literal reality behind Pynchon's symbolic "IG." See Joseph Borkin's *The Crime and Punishment of I. G. Farben* (New York: Free Press, 1978), reviewed in *New York Times Book Review*, Aug. 6, 1978.

21. Cf. Wordsworth:
> This City now doth, like a garment, wear
> The beauty of the morning; silent, bare,
> Ships, towers, domes, theaters, and temples lie
> Open unto the fields, and to the sky;
> All bright and glittering in the smokeless air.

22. *Knowledge and Wonder* (Garden City, N.Y.: Doubleday, 1966), pp. 227–28.

Five

Reading Pynchon

Prose at the Interface

> "As long as you stay always right
> at the edge between fair lowlands
> and the madness of Donar it does
> not fail you, whatever it is that
> flies, this carrying drive toward—
> *is* it freedom?"

Pynchon's characters live in the conditional ground between the facts of their Situations and what the meaning of those facts may be. Readers of Pynchon's writing occupy that same uncertain ground because the stories he tells do not resolve in ways that align form with meaning. Ideas within his fiction and the forms of his fiction are kept in a skewed relation, so that meaning is only obliquely related to the direction of a plot line, the outcome of a character, or the late arrival of some discovery that clarifies the whole. Because plots are the form of meaning, Pynchon's unresolved plots frustrate the attempt to distill meaning from them. Moreover, Pynchon's heavy reliance upon ideas compounds the reader's confusion, for ideas are the near relative of meaning, which is their structure, and their fecund presence invites readers to seek the consistency and pattern which would give that presence form and provide a stable point of view. Patterns abound, but without consistency; as a result, the ideas which proliferate throughout Pynchon's narrative world are as much things in that world as they are possible meanings of it. And therefore, like the figures within the fiction, readers are stalled at the interface between the facts—the printed words—and what those facts may mean.

This experience in the reading of Pynchon's writing is the result of a conscious narrative strategy on his part to engage readers in the activity and condition of meaning. Meaning in Pynchon is always a medium, not an answer; his goal is to induce that medium, verging on psychosis, whereby the sterile and false world of "official" forms is given the lie by a protective and inquisitive alertness, leaving an uncertain reality which both terrifies and releases. If his characters were able to clutch what they seek in the world, that found reality would lose its power and value as a source of meaning for their world. For the reader too, then, the threshold is the proper relation to meaningfulness. Given, "official" facts despiritualize, but facts which may hold the key to a reality or understanding beyond themselves are a source of animation. This is both the reason and the importance of Pynchon's conditional prose at the interface.

In his discussion of plot Aristotle directs our attention precisely to the threshold which characterizes Pynchon's stylistic intentions: "Even matters of chance seem most marvellous if there is an appearance of design as it were in them; as for instance the statue of Argos killed the author of Mitys' death by falling down on him when a looker-on at a public spectacle; for incidents like that we think to be not without meaning. A plot therefore, of this sort is necessarily finer than others."[1] By comparison, when Oedipa Maas drives into San Narciso for the first time, she is reminded by that town's "ordered swirl of houses and streets" of a radio's printed circuit she had once seen, for "there were to both outward patterns a hieroglyphic sense of concealed meaning, of an intent to communicate. . . . She and the Chevy seemed parked at the centre of an odd religious instant" (13).

The comparison of the two passages shows how a specific stylistic device achieves specific thematic goals, for Oedipa's experience here (and throughout the book) is conveyed in a style which gives "matters of chance" the "appearance of design." Furthermore, because of the proximity of the narrator's voice to Oedipa's thoughts, the reader experiences with her the threshold sense of "concealed meaning." As in Aristotle's example of coincidence, both Oedipa and the reader think the patterns "to be not without meaning." Oedipa gives sacred connotations to this meaning, for she "seemed parked at the centre of an odd religious instant." This experience of the sacred in the midst of the profane Mircea Eliade has called "hierophany."[2]

As in the experience of hierophany described by Eliade, Oedipa's experience of meaning is unsure; this lack of certainty, this dwelling between profane and sacred interpretations, characterizes Pynchon's stylistic intentions and their relation to his subject matter. That relation reveals itself in the uncertain, provisional behavior of his style. In the passage above, from *The Crying of Lot 49*, it is best exemplified by the careful use of the word "seemed" and the identity of perspective shared by narrator, character, and reader. Pynchon provides no additional, inside information about Oedipa's situation. This style generates a tension between the opposing worlds it implicates and joins (suburban swirl : sacred text), and it is this stylistic tension that positions characters and reader alike at the interface between opposite views of the same event.

What is at issue here is precisely the uncertainty of the event's meaning. The correct interpretation of the statue's falling (in Aristotle's example), or of Oedipa's hieroglyphic patterns, remains undetermined and hangs between indifferent chance and sacred design. The location between the two is the locus of both Oedipa's and the reader's thoughts.

Aristotle's discussion of the well-made plot (literary craft) is congruent with Pynchon's thematic concern with plotting (literary subject matter). Were Aristotle to read *The Crying of Lot 49*, he would be attentive to the plausibility of Oedipa's driving to San Narciso in the first place; why events of the plot happen in succession is his concern. If they so happen both unexpectedly and in consequence, as they do in Oedipus's unmasking, it is a good plot. Aristotle's inclusion in his commentary of "the appearance of design" permits events of the plot to be linked by fitness, irony, and meaningfulness, and here Pynchon fulfills the requirement of linkage. The difference between their notions of plot which is relevant here is that Aristotle's concern with plot is from the *outside* (as reader, critic, and audience), whereas that concern in Pynchon becomes a metaphor for the difficulty of knowing from the *inside* whether or not a set of events constitutes a designed plot or is merely coincidental. Pynchon's writing, moreover, engages both concerns; the events of his plots which puzzle the characters inside them are conveyed in a style which presents the reader, outside, with the same enigmas.

Tzvetan Todorov's structural definition of the "fantastic" as a genre proceeds directly from a point co-terminous with Aristotle's remarks, for the "fantastic" is that "hesitation: between two understandings of the same experience." In Todorov this hesitation is always between a natural explanation ("illusion of the senses," "product of the imagination") in which the "laws of the universe . . . remain what they are," and a supernatural explanation, in which "reality is controlled by laws unknown to us." The essence of the genre, however, is the "hesitation": "The fantastic occupies the duration of this uncertainty." Moreover, "the fantastic . . . implies an integration of the reader into the world of the characters; that world is defined by the reader's own ambiguous perception of the events narrated."[3]

Hesitation and uncertainty in Pynchon's fiction are of a far more varied origin than that described by Todorov (who draws largely upon gothic horror fiction). In Pynchon's writing "the appearance of design" may well be taken as sign of "another order of being," but this order has its origins as often in political, social, and personal plotting as it does in any supernatural agency.

Pynchon establishes that uncertainty stylistically. His reasons for doing so are made evident as early as *V.*, where metaphor is an "artifice . . . cloaking . . . innate mindlessness" (305). Pynchon knows that he is using metaphor to say even that much; this paradox, implicit in Maijstral's journal entry, is made explicit in *The Crying of Lot 49*, where the literate heroine realizes "the act of metaphor then was a thrust at truth and a lie, depending where you were: inside, safe, or outside, lost" (95). These two passages document an advance in his conception, for Oedipa's reflections stress the "act" of language and insist upon the bridging character of metaphor.

Pynchon's preoccupation with metaphor makes sense, for the act of metaphor establishes meaning by bridging the gap between event and meaning. Pynchon's narratives purposely avoid completing the metaphoric act because he is after the intimation of meaning, not its dogmatic assertion. He wants to create suspicion and paranoia, not confident conviction and belief. Thus, in the example with which we began, the metaphor of "religious instant" (that is, the instant *is* religious, the patterns *are* a sacred text) is arrested and left incomplete by the persistent use of conditional words such as "seemed," "as if," "perhaps," and "either . . . or." By arresting the reader between chance and the appearance of design, Pynchon's style generates the titillating intimations of what in *Gravity's Rainbow* will become the explicit and equally ambiguous references to "another order."

Pynchon's stylistic devices, therefore, have specific thematic goals, and both are inseparable from each other; the provisional character of his style throws into jeopardy the meanings his subject matter may have for the reader, and the uncertainty itself is one of his subjects. The conditional mode of the narrator's voice in *The Crying of Lot 49* matches the "as if" confusion in Oedipa's hesitant understanding; the difficulty of remaining at this interface, of maintaining the ground between her profane culture on the one hand, and the possibilities of its meanings on the other, is one theme of that book. More generally, that interface is the stylistic intention of all Pynchon's writing, and is not a denial of the possibility of meaning, or of the connections between experience and meaning, so much as it is an insistence that meaningfulness requires uncertainty. For Pynchon to affirm directly that Oedipa's experience is mystical or religious, or that Tristero exists literally, would be to change the entire nature of the book and reduce the importance of her adventures. Such an affirmation would mean only that she had found a secret enclave, instead of an exact and rigorous relationship between her culture and her understanding of it.

This relationship is rigorous because it encompasses opposites which refuse to resolve. The underworld Oedipa "discovers" is "congruent with the cheered land" (135). This coincidence of meanings and worlds at all points (superposable, correspondent), inside and outside, in the street and under the street, Callisto above and Meatball below, is characteristic of Pynchon's writing, from an early story such as "Entropy" to *Gravity's Rainbow*. Throughout, the reader is kept between those points which coincide, all of which exist in Pynchon's art on the same vertical axis of imagination.

Such coincidence of opposites is a characteristic of hierophany, as Eliade insists: "It is impossible to overemphasize the paradox represented by every hierophany. . . . By manifesting the sacred, any object becomes *something else*, yet it continues to remain *itself*."[4] Sacred and profane are congruent; Pynchon plays on this correspondence by finding in the most ludicrous that which is most important. This underlies the cavalier manner in which Pynchon places the profane Americanism "to park" (and its cultural vehicle, the Chevy) next to "sacred instant." The entire book pulses with this paradox, as it should, for its theme is paradoxical. In a world of mass communication, true community is rare, even illegal, as implied in Pynchon's allusive legalism, "an intent to communicate."

Pynchon's style, then, opens up a space between chance and design, experience and meaning, and the profane and the sacred. This space between is at the same time a conjunction and an intersection. Eliade calls it the locus of "hierophany," Todorov the "fantastic," and Aristotle (less directly) the "marvelous." This style determines the way in which readers view the subjects of Pynchon's plots and keeps the plots suspended without resolution. As such, his style is a model of consciousness and expresses a relation to the world which Pynchon forces upon the reader in the act of reading.

In *Gravity's Rainbow* Pynchon's stylistic intentions are furthered by the use of the Poisson distribution. The novel begins with fear of the V-2 rocket. Pirate Prentice dreams of evacuation and awakes to see the vapor trail of a V-2 over the English Channel; we are soon introduced to Lt. Slothrop, who investigates bomb sites, and to Roger Mexico, who plots their distribution. The V-bomb distribution is one of the most well-known examples of a Poisson distribution. Pynchon may have read about it in an introductory statistics course at Cornell University.[5] A footnote in Feller's *An Introduction to Probability Theory* refers his readers to the *Journal of the Institute of Actuaries* and a brief one-page article by R. D. Clarke, F.I.A., of the Prudential Assurance Company, Ltd., entitled "An Application of the Poisson Distribution." Clarke recalls: "During the flying-bomb attack on London, frequent assertions were made that the points of impact of the bombs tended to be grouped in clusters. It was accordingly decided to apply a statistical test to discover whether any support could be found for this allegation." This amounts to the creation of such a map as Roger Mexico's. Clarke concluded: "The result provided a very neat example of conformity to the Poisson law and might afford material to future writers of statistical text-books" for "the closeness of fit which in fact appears lends no support to the clustering hypothesis."[6] Feller apparently followed Clarke's suggestion, and concluded his own discussion of the flying-bomb example with these striking words: "We have here an instructive illustration of the established fact that to the untrained eye randomness appears as regularity or tendency to cluster."[7]

The aptness of the Poisson distribution for Pynchon's intentions is remarkable, for the equation literally joins randomness with regularity. And here, perhaps, it is most forcefully brought home how inseparable are Pynchon's stylistic intentions and the subject of that intent. The Poisson equation is a mathematical paradigm for the vexing oppositions which vacillate throughout *Gravity's Rainbow*, for the equation "interfaces" two opposing views of the world: one which sees all things as determined (if the rockets' distribution is the revelation of some Design, "we'll have shown again the stone determinacy of everything," *GR*, 86), and the other view which sees events as accidental ("That's the Monte Carlo Fallacy. No matter how many have fallen inside a particular square, the odds remain the same as they always were," *GR*, 56).

The Poisson distribution law is a mathematical description of randomness; as such, it seems to embody in itself the opposite of what it describes.[8] Pynchon's prose creates the interface between those opposites which the equation joins, as this passage shows: "Only a classical Poisson distribution, quietly neatly sifting among the squares exactly as it should . . . growing to its predicted shape . . ." (56). The narrator here undermines the randomness he pretends to assert by intimating through the use of ellipsis and personification that there is nonetheless some Design buried within the disinterested distribution.

Moreover, the ominous and stealthy behavior attributed to the "predicted shape" as it sifts and grows reminds the reader that this chapter began with sinister language: "Something's stalking through the city of Smoke" (53). This is the lexicon of fear, just as these early chapters are chapters of fear, portraying a city and a people under attack from a missile that gives no warning. But that fear, recreated stylistically, is transformed into the paranoid, uncertain humor of these wartime scenes, whose immediate dramatic purpose is the evocation of the fear, paranoia, and uncertainty which afflicts the characters. Fear is the emotional expression of their uncertainty; the "operational paranoia" which suffuses the narrative voice as well as a good part of the dialogue of *Gravity's Rainbow* is the appropriate stylistic expression and vehicle for the indeterminacy which grips the characters' lives. The style, then, always serves at least the two purposes of dramatizing the characters' uncertainty and positioning the reader between the opposing possibilities aligned on either side of that uncertainty.

Because the Poisson law is misunderstood by Pointsman, he tries to use it as a hedge against his own fear, for the law gives the "appearance of design" to the terrible War and the "absolute rule of chance" (96). But this law for the lawless only provides appearance, not certainty; Pointsman remains at the interface. Pointsman tries to pull reality to one side of this boundary by showing its obedience to cause-and-effect determinism. He cannot understand how Mexico can "play, so at his ease, with these symbols of randomness and fright," and wonders if "Postwar will be nothing but 'events,' newly created one moment to the next? No links? Is it the end of history?" (56).

Pointsman's misery articulates another example of the polarity in both style and theme being discussed here. The opposition between "events" and "history" is a further expression of the uncertainty which obtains between unencumbered facts and the meanings ("history") those facts may represent. This particular expression of that uncertainty is especially important for our understanding of Pynchon's stylistic intentions; on the one hand, he may be said to have the unveiling of "underground" history as his ideological motive, while on the other, he is adamantly opposed, stylistically, to the creation of any stable, fixed "history." Pynchon describes the pathology of historical events while fighting the inherent tendency of his medium (the printed word) to present such description as explanation.

In the dying pages of *V.* we are with Sidney Stencil, in the days of an earlier "Postwar":

Wasn't the armistice signed by legally constituted heads of government? How could there not be peace? It would never be worth the trouble arguing. So they'd stood that November morning, watching the lamp-lighter extinguish the lights in St. James's Park, as if having long ago passed through some quicksilver surface from when Viscount Grey had stood perhaps at the same window and made his famous remark about the lamps going out all over Europe. Stencil of course didn't see the difference between event and image, but saw no advantage in disturbing the chief's euphoria. (431)

Eventually, Sidney's clarity succumbs to the lure of the Past and he falls to one side of the interface of "the real present." This concept, which he used to embody, becomes a nostalgic memory; he "belonged to a time where the side a man was on didn't matter, only the state of opposition itself." This, he feels, is preferable to a belief in the Future: "this loathsome weakness of retreat into dreams: pastel visions of disarmament, a League, a universal law" (431).

The opposition between Sidney Stencil (the Past) and his boss, Carruthers-Pillow (who believes in the Future), is the time-bound fulcrum of *V.*'s timeless structure. Nothing is more distinctive of Pynchon's writing than this congruent polarity in both subject and style, which locates characters and readers at the interface. His early story "Entropy" is a clear visual example of that interface, for the text itself alternates between two spaces: Callisto's hermetic apartment and Meatball's open party. The alternating presentation of the two spaces (and the ideas attached to each) places the reader directly in a third space between the two apartments and what they mean. A neat, thematic example of the same opposition is summarized in Stencil's "political moral" (cited above, p. 11) near the end of *V.*:

"we carry on the business of this century with an intolerable double vision. Right and Left; the hothouse and the street. The Right can only live and work hermetically, in the hothouse of the past, while outside the Left prosecute their affairs in the streets by manipulated mob violence. And cannot but live in the dreamscape of the future.

"What of the real present, the men-of-no-politics, the once-respectable Golden Mean? Obsolete; in any case, lost sight of. In a West of such extremes we can expect, at the very least, a highly 'alienated' populace within not many more years." (440)

The polarity which creates and bounds that alienation is the persistent characteristic of Pynchon's style, from passages such as the one above in *V.*, to the marvelous prose of the "excluded middle" in *The Crying of Lot 49*, to the "Basic Two" of *Gravity's Rainbow*. It has been his equally persistent intention to locate both characters and readers within the interstices of those polarities.

To imagine that Pynchon would allow us beyond those interior spaces is folly, for his narrative strategy is designed to create a threshold experience. If, at this threshold, life is unsure and only possibly meaningful; if we are alone there and alienated from our cultural community; and if, without the illusion of answers, we fear what may happen—at least life at the threshold has the impact of meaning; at least we share with Oedipa in the anti-community of our mutual isolation; and if there is fear, so is there something within us that must "leap and sing" (*GR*, 396). Like any medium, Pynchon coerces us into a way of perceiving; his effort is always to keep the reader at the interface, where the facts of his fiction possess the intriguing and disturbing reality of signs.

The Seductions of Fact

> "Really, universally, relations stop nowhere, and the exquisite problem of the artist is eternally but to draw, by a geometry of his own, the circle within which they shall happily *appear* to do so."
> Henry James, "Preface" to *Roderick Hudson*

> "Every natural fact is a symbol of some spiritual fact."
> Ralph Waldo Emerson, "Nature"

Readers of Pynchon sympathize with Oedipa's loneliness at the end of *The Crying of Lot 49*, for Pynchon's artistic intentions are the reverse of James's. Pynchon's problem is to avoid closure, not to invent it. His presentation of facts must imply without asserting, so that the facts are released from the rational structures of stable (and false) meaning without supplying at the same time another systematic restructuring which is equally pernicious. As a result, readers are confronted with texts whose meanings are never fixed, and they experience the severe loneliness of continuities that are discontinuous (though congruent) with the literal reality of the words which prompted them.

Like Oedipa, the reader has only words. They are the facts in the world of Pynchon's fiction and hang like signs between the world of meaning intended by his fiction and the world of the reader. That is, the words are not merely the passive medium of the world they create but an aggressive message-system congruent with it. In *The Crying of Lot 49*, for example, the reader begins to suffer from a paranoid watchfulness long before it afflicts Oedipa. The call letters of Mucho's radio station, "KCUF," are a joke some reviewers found in bad taste,[9] but the letters are part of Pynchon's strategy to induce in the reader an inquisitive alertness congruent with the blossoming paranoia of the book's heroine. The call letters present the reader with a set of questions which parallel those facing Oedipa: are these letters arbitrary or purposeful? have they a literal meaning directly linked to specific plot and character, or are they relevant only within the complex of meaning of the book? The letters are never questioned within the novel. They may be an oblique commentary on Mucho's situation, or his weakness for "chicks," but their primary purpose is to call attention to themselves and raise the possibility that the text itself may be only a tasteless joke or a code promising a meaningful world.

The meanings which words may have in Pynchon's writing are multiple and related, so that the reader, like Oedipa, is engulfed by meaning. We begin to suspect, with her, that there is "revelation in progress" everywhere in the novel. When Oedipa woke Metzger in her motel room at the Echo Courts, "his radiant eyes flew open, pierced her" (26); Pynchon's choice of the word "pierced" invokes the will of Pierce Inverarity that has penetrated her life, the kind of stamps he collected, the impalement of Turks and New Zealanders then occurring on the TV screen before them, the sexual penetration which is about to occur, as well as the underlying theme of feedback and the closed system which the book enacts. This invocation of meanings overwhelms the immediate moment in the story and creates that dissonance between meaning and fact which borders on farce, just as the meanings attached to Slothrop far outweigh his literal existence as a character.

This aspect of Pynchon's strategy is especially evident in the choice of a word whose first appearance calls attention to itself, as does the word "bloom" when the image of Baby Igor "bloomed" onto the screen of the TV (17). But the word "bloom" is one of the most oft-repeated words in this echoing book, and quickly becomes associated with Oedipa's education and "the languid, sinister blooming of The Tristero" (36). Pynchon's technique plays on the repetitions of words until they assume to themselves alarming and unmanageable corporations of meaning; this repetition of words "conditions" the reader to an almost psychotic awareness. When the narrator stops to summarize Oedipa's plight after she leaves John Nefastis, the reader is prepared for the undertones resonating beneath the text: "Now here was Oedipa, faced with a metaphor of God knew how many parts" (80). Buried beneath the idiomatic surface of Oedipa's reflection is, perhaps, a textual hint that she faces simply a "metaphor of God."

Pynchon's texts, like the Tristero, continue to bloom the more we pursue them. Their reality is latent rather than fully present. That is, the correspondence of the world in the fiction to the world of the reader is not immediately apparent, but the more pursuit the reader gives to the text, the more the relation between the worlds becomes established, binding, and inseparable. Most authors who flood their books with facts drawn from the reader's world do so in an effort to create the illusion of realism and gain credibility for their plots and characters. Melville, for example, insists repeatedly in *Moby-Dick* that the events he relates are "by no means unprecedented." By contrast, the first effect of Pynchon's facts is the violation of plausibility. The Thurn and Taxis postal system sounds as unlikely as "Genghis Cohen"; the parapsychological hijinks of *Gravity's Rainbow* seem to be a fanciful extension of Nefastian spiritualism. Yet, a little checking discovers that these are oddities of the reader's world and not fictions of Pynchon's imagination.[10]

Pynchon uses the Thurn and Taxis postal system in *The Crying of Lot 49* as the historical axis he needs to establish the temporal dimension of the congruence Oedipa finds, but the old European postal organization is so little known by most readers that his use of it seems to be an example of esoterica. Yet this is but another instance of Pynchon's effort to open up and multiply history. Pynchon has recorded accurately the facts of the once powerful postal monopoly, including its use of the badger skin and the post horn symbol. Indeed, according to Ernst Puttkammer's *Princes of Thurn and Taxis* (1938), the post horn "is to this day the symbol on Continental Europe of the postal organization."[11]

Pynchon's use of this fact, in other words, is part of his project to propagate and multiply relations; his verbal repetitions and coincidences help create a fabric of meaning which duplicates the cross-purposes of the historical process. The success of the Thurn and Taxis system, for example, rested in part upon the coincidental fact that the word "Taxis" is the German equivalent of the Italian "tasso" meaning "badger." Badger skins, as Puttkammer explains, were believed to be talismans against evil, and each courier therefore "had to have his bit of badger skin showing prominently." This superstition began to die out, but "by an amusing and yet obvious mistake, all couriers were soon thought to be carrying the emblem (I almost might say the trade mark) of our Tassi family."[12]

Puttkammer's book reads in places like the historical section of *The Crying of Lot 49* (116–31). The family acquired a monopoly on the courier business which proved so profitable that competing messenger services sought to disrupt their post. In the Low Countries especially "the cities set up their own competing messenger services and answered laws forbidding them by regularly beating up the Taxis messengers."[13] Niccolo's death in Wharfinger's *The Courier's Tragedy*, which Oedipa attends in chapter three, grows less fictional and more "curious" as the connections between the facts of Pynchon's world and ours multiply. As the reality of Thurn and Taxis mushrooms, so grows the apparition of Tristero. We are seduced, like Oedipa, by the "logic" of it. When the family was accorded nobility, its coat of arms carried the post horn emblem, which Puttkammer notes was about as "subtle as if Mr. William Wrigley were accorded one of a stick of gum crossed by a baseball bat." Correspondingly, it makes sense that a competing messenger service (such as the Tristero) should have as its "iconography the muted post horn and a dead badger with its four feet in the air (some said that the name Taxis came from the Italian *tasso*, badger, referring to hats of badger fur the early Bergemascan couriers wore)" (*CL49*, 120).

The real world of the reader is part of Pynchon's fiction; the two, which at first seem so far apart, become inseparable in the act of informed reading. The reader is the Demon inside Pynchon's world, sorting and "unpacking" the facts. As their overt presence within the fiction is shown to correspond to a covert presence in our world, the reader is engaged, like Oedipa, in a transvaluation of the given understandings of his world. Pynchon's narratives contain and show relations among a dizzying number of facts, and are so constituted that the reader is drawn into adding to this number, making connections he is then left to juggle into meaning, all the while wondering whose connections they are, his or Pynchon's.[14] As with Stencil and Oedipa, this is both a therapy for isolation and a threat to the clarity among facts that any understanding of them requires.

The seductive quality of Pynchon's facts derives not only from those stylistic cues which prompt the reader but also from the "Puritan reflex" of the reader. Pynchon knows that he is addressing an audience addicted to knowing, and one which believes passionately in "the facts." In this sense, Pynchon's fiction relies upon the "work" of the reader, his eagerness to read facts as symbols of another order. In particular, *Gravity's Rainbow* dramatizes how natural hope is to human consciousness and how little stimulus is required to create a positive response. In Pavlov's terminology hope is "ultraparadoxical" in *Gravity's Rainbow*, for it survives in the fairy tales, the psychic measurements, and Advent services of London under bombardment. The study and analysis of facts is a defense against uncertainty and the imminence of death.

Correspondingly, Pynchon's books are filled with so much knowledge, and flooded with so many facts and their endless relations, that they trigger in the reader a similar hopeful expectation that reading them will result in enlightenment. Pynchon uses his encyclopedic knowledge about the world and especially the nooks and crannies of history, the major arcana, underground societies, whispers toward Unity, mythic consciousness, life after death, and other portentous facts to tap the response P. W. Bridgman predicted in his 1929 article on the uncertainty principle, then recently formulated by Werner Heisenberg:

The immediate effect of the uncertainty principle will be to let loose a veritable intellectual spree of licentious and debauched thinking. This will come from the refusal to take at its true value the statement that it is meaningless to penetrate much deeper than the electron, and will have the thesis that there *is really* a domain beyond, only that man with his present limitations is not fitted to enter this domain. . . . The existence of such a domain will be made the basis of an orgy of rationalizing. It will be made the substance of the soul; . . . the principle of vital processes will have its seat here; and it will be the medium of telepathic communication. One group will find in the failure of the physical law of cause and effect the solution of the age-old problem of the freedom of the will, and, on the other hand, the atheist will find the justification of his contention that chance rules the universe.[15]

Arthur Koestler has written that physicists themselves number among the founders and members of clubs for parapsychological research.[16] Von Braun's words, which form the epigraph of *Gravity's Rainbow*, are a paradigm of the reflex being discussed here, whereby facts are taken to be promises of a beyond: "Everything science has taught me, and continues to teach me, strengthens my belief in the continuity of our spiritual existence after death."

As the irony of that epigraph makes clear, the reflex possesses a problematic value in Pynchon's writing. On the one hand, the attempt to discern the meaning of facts is the source of meaningful connection and freedom from the machinery of political and social systems that would otherwise persist unnoticed. On the other hand, such rational discernment is an example of those western traditions of analysis which have created the technological systems that keep men organized but separate and threaten all freedom. This paradox is dramatized most clearly in the narcissistic convolutions of *The Crying of Lot 49*, and its technological consequences are made plain in the exploitation of Franz Pokler and the other engineers (including von Braun) who dreamed of space travel. Readers of Pynchon's books, therefore, cannot ignore that the act of reading is itself a systematic enterprise. Because his books resist understanding, they both heighten and frustrate that enterprise.[17]

The "scholarly quests" (*V.*, 50) of Pynchon's characters and readers place his fiction at an ironic tangent to the American tradition, the roots of which are in Puritanism and which has its transcendental expression in Emerson's "Nature," which reads the world as material sign of spiritual fact. Pynchon is at some remove from that Emersonian assurance because, like Melville, he questions the certainty of that correspondence. Unlike Whitman's detailed catalogues that declare a benign fullness in which everywhere *is* meaning, Pynchon's characters, like Ahab before them, treat the world as a clue, not the thing itself; thus in *Moby-Dick* the marvelous variety of the earth presented in the narration becomes for Ahab a set of leads in the search for the White Whale. Characteristically, this becomes in Pynchon's book the futile search for the Rocket: "LOOK-IN' FAWR A NEEDLE IN A HAAAAY-STACK!" (*GR*, 561).

Both Melville and Pynchon dramatize the Puritan disposition to read the world as message and thereby to penetrate it; both demonstrate the relationship between the compulsion for religious or absolute knowledge and the growth of technology. *Moby-Dick* and *Gravity's Rainbow* describe the consequences of the systematic search for the revelation which facts seem to promise. Like *Gravity's Rainbow*, Melville's book is filled with arcana, portents, signs, and mysterious configurations. The Rocket and the Whale are the central symbols of their respective civilizations, and are used in the two books as the objects of search and analysis.

Both books are about reading texts and the systems of understanding which characters read out of their central symbols. The first word of *Moby-Dick* is "Etymology," meaning to speak the real or true. What follows immediately is the etymology of the word "whale," but this etymology only repeats what men have made of their confrontations with whaleness, and says nothing which explains the presence of the whale. The chapter "The Doubloon" is a microcosm of the attention given to the text of the whale. The narrator of this section cries: "And some certain significance lurks in all things, else all things are little worth, and the round world itself but an empty cipher." When Stubb uses an

almanac to help him decipher the doubloon, he anticipates Oedipa's despair over the word "Tristero": "Book! you lie there; the
fact is, you books must know your places. You'll do to give us the
bare words and facts, but we come in to supply the thoughts.
That's my small experience. . . . Signs and wonders, eh? Pity if
there is nothing wonderful in signs, and significant in wonders!"

The resistance of the doubloon to interpretation is characteristic of facts. One purpose of the tremendous number of facts in the
cetology chapters is the creation of whale-vision, so that the entire perception of the universe is transformed into the terms of
the whale's bulk, its very palpability. For it is Moby-Dick's mute
thingness that inspires Ahab's rage:

"All visible objects, man, are but as pasteboard masks. But in each
event—in the living act, the undoubted deed—there, some unknown
but still reasoning thing puts forth the mouldings of its features from
behind the unreasoning mask. If man will strike, strike through the
mask! How can the prisoner reach outside except by thrusting through
the wall? To me, the white whale is that wall, shoved near to me. Sometimes I think there's naught beyond. But 'tis enough. He tasks me; he
heaps me; I see in him outrageous strength, with an inscrutable malice
sinewing it. That inscrutable thing is chiefly what I hate."

Even though the cetology chapters spin the whale out "to the
uttermost coils of his bowels," the whale remains unfathomable.
No dissection can uncover the reason for the whale's existence.
The white whale is reborn (like Adams's Virgin) as Pynchon's
Rocket, and all the engineers are at its mercy: "not only danger
from explosions or falling hardware, but also its dumbness, its
dead weight, its obstinate and palpable mystery" (GR, 402).

The distinction implicit in the foregoing passages between
analysis and explanation was formulated succinctly by Wittgenstein in the Tractatus: "It is not how things are in the world that
is mystical, but that it exists" (6.44). Facts promise a bridge from
"how" to "that"; description masquerades as explanation. Both
Moby-Dick and Gravity's Rainbow are tremendous "encyclope-
dias" of "how things are in the world." Melville was criticized for
his "inartistic heaping up of details,"[18] yet such accumulation
reflects the human acquisition of fact which enables action but
does not explain being.

Such plenitude provides the hunting grounds for meaning. With *Gravity's Rainbow* the grounds have shifted from gold doubloons to aromatic heterocyclic polymers, from a technology inspired by a hatred of nature's inscrutability to a world in which technology is man's natural habitat, as inscrutable and threatening to him as the white whale is to Ahab. Both books focus on what we do with the facts, and upon our conviction that a proper analysis of them will reveal the key to the meaning of the world we so carefully examine.

Pynchon's books are full of engineers because they work at the interface between analysis and explanation. In reality, of course, that dualism is transformed into the continuity between theory and practice; "explanation" remains elusive. The motivations of the Verein für Raumschiffahrt originate in dreams of transcendence; they are engineers of poetic vision trying to complete a metaphor with a machine. They represent in *Gravity's Rainbow* both the scientific motivation to reduce the gap between "how" the world is and "that" it is, and the consequence of that drive, which is the routinization of dream. Men of science, with the charisma we bestow upon them, expedite the technological transformation of dreams into what dreams become in "our accumulated daylight" (*CL49*, 133). Science occupies in the modern world that place once held by visionary poets: they describe the universe to us, and it is their analysis of the facts which claims our belief.

Our belief, of course, is not shared by those men of science, who recognized long ago that their descriptions have an operative, technological value but are not themselves explanations of the universe. Wittgenstein, for example, who came to language philosophy from his engineering studies at Manchester, says plainly, "The whole modern conception of the world is founded on the illusion that the so-called laws of nature are the explanations of natural phenomena" (6.371). Wittgenstein in 1921 wasn't alone. Henry Adams, whose *Education* was first published in 1918, was driving a similar wedge between description and explanation. What Whitehead in 1925 in the Lowell Lectures called "scientific materialism" was dying, though the society it created has not.

Moreover, with the advent of quantum theory there enters a limitation on science's ability to communicate its descriptive knowledge. Reading in the available layman's literature on the developments in physics over the last three-quarters of a century, one is struck by a recurring theme: the physical description of the universe is no longer susceptible to expression in ordinary, everyday language. Heisenberg's *Physics and Beyond*, for example, is almost preoccupied with this fact.[19] Classical, Newtonian, physics seemed to be normative because its laws could be expressed in language which conformed to our everyday sense-impressions of the universe. The model of three-dimensional, geometrical space is also a model of the way in which our senses perceive the world. With the acceptance and use of quantum theory, however, that conformity disappears:

This is the whole paradox of quantum theory. On the one hand, we establish laws that differ from those of classical physics; on the other, we apply the concepts of classical physics quite unreservedly whenever we make observations, or take measurements or photographs. And we have to do just that because, when all is said and done, we are forced to use language if we are to communicate our results to other people. . . . We have learned that this language is an inadequate means of communication and orientation, but it is nevertheless the presupposition of all science.[20]

As early as the 1920s Niels Bohr said to Heisenberg, "When it comes to atoms, language can be used only as in poetry. The poet, too, is not nearly so concerned with describing facts as with creating images." Jacob Bronowski, writing in 1973, glosses Bohr's comment: "There is no other way to talk about the invisible—in nature, in art, or in science. When we step through the gateway of the atom, we are in a world which our senses cannot experience." In order to describe that world, we must create new images for it, but those images must "come from the concrete world of our senses, because that is the only world that words describe. But all our ways of picturing the invisible are metaphors, likenesses that we snatch from the larger world of eye and ear and touch."[21]

This realization that science, too, shares the uncertain relation between facts and what they may mean underlies Fausto Maijstral's diary entry in *V.*: "while others may look on the laws of physics as legislation," poets are "alone with the task of living in a universe of things which simply are" (305). Fausto includes in the diary a poem by his friend, the engineer-poet Dubnietna:

> If I told you the truth
> You would not believe me.
> If I said: no fellow soul
> Drops death from the air, no conscious plot
> Drove us underground, you would laugh
> As if I had twitched the wax mouth
> Of my tragic mask into a smile—
> A smile to you: to me the truth behind
> The catenary: locus of the transcendental:
> $y = a/2 \left(e^{x/a} + e^{-x/a} \right).$

The "catenary" is "the shape of the curve assumed by a uniform, heavy flexible cord freely suspended from its extremities."[22] In Dubnietna's engineering poetic, smiles are catenaries. His poem presents an unwelcome proposition for those beseiged on Malta: the bombings are not the result of conscious design but merely the way things "hang." Such a view takes the consciousness out of history and divorces events and values. It is an engineer's poetic: things happen because it is in their nature to do so; an apple falls not because someone wills it but because in this world that is what ripe apples do.

Dubnietna's "truth" is but half of the complementary vision which characterizes Pynchon's writing, for nowhere is the conscious and tragic terror of the Maltese Situation denied. Dubnietna's poem is biased but is nonetheless an ingenious balancing of the "tragic mask" which assumes a conscious fate, and the comic "smile" of indifferent chance. The two are united in the mathematical language of engineers, and this mathematical expression, denuded of human experience and value, is an early example of the threat which the engineering mind poses and which becomes so dominant in *Gravity's Rainbow*.

The poetry of mathematics divorces events from human value; the curve of life and history, expressed mathematically, is a continuity in which morality is absent. The "passage" of the Rocket symbolizes that curve, but is "reduced" by its engineers "to bourgeois terms, terms of an equation such as that elegant blend of philosophy and hardware, abstract change and hinged pivots of real metals which describes motion under the aspect of yaw control" (239). Fahringer is "the only one of the Peenemünde club who refused to wear the exclusive pheasant-feather badge in his hatband because he couldn't bring himself to kill" (454). Of all the engineers in *Gravity's Rainbow*—Achtfaden, Mondaugen, Pokler, Weissmann, Fibel, Närrisch, Flaum, Weichensteller—Fahringer alone remembers that his actions are contributing to human death. In the reduction of human scale to mathematical terms, and the specializations of technology, the others avoid that responsibility. One of the Schwarzkommando asks Achtfaden: "Do you find it a little schizoid . . . breaking a flight profile up into segments of responsibility? It was half bullet, half arrow. *It* demanded this, we didn't. So. . . . You are either alone absolutely, alone with your own death, or you take part in the larger enterprise, and you share in the deaths of others" (453–54).

Insofar as the language of science permits this segmentation (Wordsworth said "dissects"), it fosters the divorce of technique and value and aids in the creation of a technology that perpetuates the seductive and illusory promise of facts. Pynchon's books dramatize that danger and recognize that all languages (all systems, models of thought), though limited, may operate without constraint. Because of that recognition, Pynchon has consciously avoided building fiction which presents any systematic understanding. Value, for Pynchon, always lies at the interface among systems, where choices continue to be made, where there is uncertainty, and where if we value anything at all, it is because that is the way we want it to be.

Listening to Pynchon: The Orphic Voice and Value among Fragments

> "Listen to this mock-angel singing"

Pynchon's writing places us with Sidney Stencil at the uncertain interface of the multiple dimensions which create the Situation, but Pynchon's voice, over the course of his three novels, is increasingly "everywhere." The line between *V.* and *Gravity's Rainbow* traces a development in Pynchon's writing from the relative stability of his presence behind *V.* to the Orphic presence of his voice in *Gravity's Rainbow*. This voice is omnipresent but not omniscient; it is a fragmented voice that is everywhere at once and so speaks, as it should, in the present tense, insisting on the Orphic fluidity of the world as process in the river of time. Pynchon has always sought in his writing a fiction aligned with the four-dimensional world-suffusion of "cross-purposes" that compose reality. For this he has developed a prose style that leaches and percolates, seeps and flushes through the dimensions of *Gravity's Rainbow*.

The fragmentation of that voice in the last one hundred pages of *Gravity's Rainbow* is the narrative counterpart to Slothrop's dissolution and, like that dissolution, balances between the clarity of false structure and the meaningful confusion of fiction-all-at-once. Because all vision is fragmentary, Pynchon has moved toward a fiction which expresses the wholeness found in the relations among fragments rather than in a false whole. Assembly must be a constant act. The harp Tyrone loses down the toilet represents his "silver chances of song" swallowed by the white symbol of rational man's fear of decay and death. But in Pynchon's Orphic song the harp is returned to Slothrop, for "there are harpmen and dulcimer players in all the rivers, wherever water moves" (622).

What chances for song there are depend upon the reader, for "the spirits of lost harpmen" must be found and made "audible" (622). Without our cooperation, the ultimate fate of the Orphic voice would be identical with Tyrone's. The continuity of a "story" makes sense but is an illusory wholeness distinct from readers. The fragmented voice is free from the oppressive implications of narrative convention, but represents a continuity which, in its extreme expression, is unintelligible. The two extremes are kept in tension by the act of reading and seeking relations among parts. This is the benign aspect of our study and participates not so much in the "routinization" of Pynchon's writing as in the community conjured by his song.

In his development from a silent presence behind *V.* to the "audible" song of *Gravity's Rainbow*, Pynchon replaces the statement of fragmentation with its example. Sidney Stencil's coherent understanding of how far beyond him the Situation is becomes Slothrop's unconscious wandering in the Zone, himself a dismembered fragment among the fragments of a destroyed world. But those fragments are important, because "in each of these streets, some vestige of humanity, of Earth, has to remain" (693). This is Pynchon speaking, in the piece of his fictional world titled "Streets," asking if in "learning to cherish what was lost, mightn't we find some way back?" Slothrop is here too, and finds in "a scrap of newspaper headline" the story of Hiroshima's disassembly. The medium is the message in these torn streets; there is no way back, save through the melodic wholeness that song has always brought to parts.

Concomitant with the growth of Pynchon's voice is a decreasing dependence upon any semblance of sequential plot. This is a natural result of Orphic speech, for the narrative order of plot lines belongs to the white, systematic world which in Pynchon's view has been responsible for so much fragmentation. The absence of "historical structure" (624), however, makes tremendous demands upon the reader. *Gravity's Rainbow* is a massive book requiring massive energies of integration. Part of this is purely a question of memory, for meaning in *Gravity's Rainbow* increasingly proceeds unaided by structure, unattached to character or event. The second sentence of the book, for example ("It has happened before, but there is nothing to compare it to now"), initiates a syntactical expectation which isn't fulfilled for twenty-six pages: "'Like a meteor shower,' they said, 'Like cinders from the Fourth of July . . .' it was 1931, and those were the comparisons" *then* (29). Not many readers, first time through, are going to pick that up, so that the book's considerable complexity is due in part to the simple fact that the elements of *Gravity's Rainbow* are all present to Pynchon. He can hold them together, because they are together for him. The space between "now" and the implied "then" is but one of many miniature arcs that Pynchon inscribes. He doesn't want to complete that arc until he has introduced Slothrop and the Puritan iconography of God's hand, but it is a connection visible only to those readers so familiar with the book that they remember it.

The demands on memory increase throughout the book. Again, this is partially for the simple reason that *Gravity's Rainbow* is a huge book with over three hundred characters. But the fragmented sections of the "nonstop revue" (681) magnify the difficulty, for mnemonic structures are almost wholly absent. These sections are fragments of speech from "the Other Side," but they are only the most starkly nonserial bits in the book, and they possess considerable thematic relevance and unity. Many of these sections refer to each other and to characters and places elsewhere in the book, but at this point the voice has abandoned the effort to enforce a narrative line. Pynchon is speaking from the vantage of the authorial present where succession in time ceases to matter and meaning overwhelms fact. The continuities here, therefore, are those of image and theme, which are well established in the first three books of the novel. Blicero's "Räumen" is simultaneous with the air-raid siren which Zhlubb hears in the prior section twenty-eight years "later." What joins the two sections is the symbol of the Rocket, and the meanings which have become attached to it.

The growth of Pynchon's voice is evident as well in the awesome power and virtuosity of his style. The closing pages of *The Crying of Lot 49* represent an advance over the choppy, slapstick prose of *V.*, and provide some hint of the rhetorical power to come. By the time of *Gravity's Rainbow* Pynchon is in possession of a dazzling range of style, from his burlesque slapstick (" 'Too young!' he screams") to romance ("You move from dream to dream inside me") to the book's dominant mood of elegy, which conveys—among others—the story of Pokler's loss: "Child phantom—white whistling, tears never to come, range the wind behind the wall. Twists of faded crepe paper blow along the ground, scuttling over his old shoes" (398).

Pynchon is a master of the dramatic scene. His Orphic voice finds and sings disparate fragments of character and event in *Gravity's Rainbow* and, particularly in the first two books of the novel, gives to each fragment the rhythm and imagery of a "whole" bit. *Gravity's Rainbow* is a series of such scenes which gathers coherence as we make out the relationships among characters, their common places of work, their designs on one another, and the fears they share. This kind of linkage begins to break down when Slothrop gives Pointsman's plot the slip in the second book, "*Un Perm' au Casino Hermann Goering*," and the novel itself turns toward the picaresque through the attention it pays to Slothrop's meanderings.

By the time this narrative fragmentation begins, Pynchon has already demonstrated his ability to exploit character, action, and image to establish tremendous wholeness in the novel. Book 2 begins at the Casino Hermann Goering and concerns Slothrop's growing awareness that what he took to be chance is really predetermined. The continuity of this section is initiated by the title, for "casino" is a game of chance. Pynchon immediately introduces the imagery of gulls in a marvelous interpenetration of the opposition between chance and determinism which permeates his book: "Up in the wind is a scavenging of gulls, sliding, easy, side to side, wings hung out still, now and then a small shrug, only to gather lift for this weaving, unweaving, white and slow faro shuffle off invisible thumbs" (181). Slothrop, a "gull" himself, is beneath these birds on his balcony. The birds become symbolic of a structure moving through them, inherent in apparent randomness, reminding readers, perhaps, of the conviction Einstein threw up to the quantum theorists, "God does not play at dice."[23] In the next twenty-two pages Slothrop saves Katje from Grigori the octopus, loses Tantivy, and has his identification papers stolen from him. In the game room of the casino he begins to understand "there is another enterprise here." Outside, he is still beneath the birds: "he heads down toward the quay, among funseekers, swooping white birds, an incessant splat of seagull shit" (203).[24]

In the narrative clarity and skill of this scene, Pynchon's voice is used to tell a story, but there are other scenes as unified where the unity proceeds directly from the voice itself, speaking to us. Pynchon as Orphic singer is fully present in the Advent scene, which begins when Roger and Jessica come upon an Advent service being held in a church in Kent. The scene begins as story but soon modulates to oratory: "The church is as cold as the night outside. There's the smell of damp wool, of bitter on the breaths of these professionals, of candle smoke and melting wax, of smothered farting, of hair tonic, of the burning oil itself, folding the other odors in a maternal way, more closely belonging to Earth, to deep strata, other times, and listen . . . listen: this is the War's evensong, the War's canonical hour, and the night is real" (129–30). Here the service within the story becomes the occasion for Pynchon's elegiac elaboration of the connections in his vision of War's arrival and the signs of its Advent. The birth this voice articulates is the transformation of toothpaste tubes into "castings, bearings, gasketry, hidden smokeshriek linings the children of that other domestic incarnation will never see. Yet the continuity, flesh to kindred metals, home to hedgeless sea, has persisted" (130). The scene returns after six pages to the Kent church where it is rounded off by the now ironic swell of the choral *"praise be to God!"* and the direct second-person address to the reader bitterly criticizing how insufficient that choral "cry" is "for you to take back to your war-address, your war-identity, across the snow's footprints and tire tracks finally to the path you must create by yourself, alone in the dark" (136).

Pynchon's Orphic song, springing from the streams of transformation, has always dwelled on the connections and continuities of loss and separation. On the bus Esther takes on her way to Schoenmaker and her nose job, a radio broadcasts Tchaikovsky's *Romeo and Juliet:* "having taken passage through transducers, coils, capacitors and tubes to a shuddering paper cone, the eternal drama of love and death continued to unfold entirely disconnected from this evening and place" (*V.*, 83). But the connection is made through the speaking voice, just as Profane and Rachel do "meet" when Pynchon tells us that she "passed by the spot" Profane had "abandoned, on her way home" (34). Pynchon, like Oedipa drinking Cohen's dandelion wine, is singing "a land where you could somehow walk, and not need the East San Narciso Freeway, and bones still could rest in peace, nourishing ghosts of dandelions, no one to plow them up. As if the dead really do persist, even in a bottle of wine" (*CL49*, 72).

Pynchon's fragmentary song insists upon continuities his singing establishes, but in *Gravity's Rainbow* the voice addresses us directly and requires our collaboration. Pynchon is less interested in "story" and what the story is about than he is in the continuity between speaker and listener. Early in the book the narrative voice speaks to Pointsman and the reader simultaneously: "You have waited in these places into the early mornings, synced into the on-whitening of the interior, you know the Arrivals schedule by heart" (50). Whenever the narrator adopts this second-person address, the tone becomes meditative, nightmarish, oratorical. The reader inevitably feels himself to be the object of this address: we become Pointsman for a few pages, or that part of us which is

Pointsman feels the accusation. The comfort we were feeling, sitting back and listening to the narrator tell his story, is lost. The separation and distance of "story" are gone; the reader-narrator-character triangle has collapsed, and we might be in a pew at some Puritan church, feeling the bite of a Doomsday sermon.[25]

The closest earlier example of this in American fiction is Hawthorne's address to Governor Pyncheon in the *The House of the Seven Gables:*

Up, therefore, Judge Pyncheon, up! You have lost a day. But tomorrow will be here anon. Will you rise, betimes, and make the most of it? Tomorrow! Tomorrow! Tomorrow! We, that are alive, may rise betimes tomorrow. As for him that has died today, his tomorrow will be the resurrection morn. . . . And how looks it now? There is no window! There is no face! An infinite, inscrutable blackness has annihilated sight! Where is our universe? All crumbled away from us; and we, adrift in chaos, may hearken to the gusts of homeless wind, that go sighing and murmuring about, in quest of what was once a world!

Pynchon's voice, like Hawthorne's, is a voice that hovers between worlds; the judge's death is a doorway making possible Hawthorne's direct confrontation of the reader with the chaos threatening us all. Characters such as Judge Pyncheon and Tyrone Slothrop are used to put readers in touch with contexts of which the characters are only minimally aware. The important pages on "Paranoid Systems of History" (238–39) are presented to us through a "revery" of Slothrop's. But this is not done through a stream of consciousness, nor is it asserted that Tyrone is dreaming such and such, but that dream puts us in touch with another order or network of meaning to which the revery is only tangential. The matter at hand in this example is Tyrone's nascent sense of a Control hovering over him, but in the pages which follow, the revery is not precisely what Tyrone thinks but what his revery puts him in touch with. And Pynchon does this because the focus is not upon Tyrone's inner psychology but upon the communal psychology of the Orphic voice and what it has to tell us.

In *The Crying of Lot 49* the second person is used by Oedipa to criticize herself: "You live in this country. You let it happen" (112). But here in *Gravity's Rainbow* the words are Pynchon's and they are spoken directly to us. The use of the second person is frequent throughout the book. When Gottfried is strapped into the Imipolex shroud, the omnipresent voice speaks to both Gottfried and the reader; the irony of its parental solace plucks at us: "Come, wake. All is well" (754). In the last section of the novel, "Descent," there is no one else in the theatre to listen but the reader.

The use of the second-person address is only the most direct way in which Pynchon's manipulation of pronouns draws us into the flow of his Orphic world. One fragment begins, "In Germany, as the end draws upon us" (72); another moves us into pre-War time with him as he remembers "the chalky walls of Mediterranean streets we quietly cycled through in noontimes of the old peace" (102). This voice has the effect of moving us through time as if it were space (which it is), and disregards the world of one-way time inherent in the white grammar of verb tenses. The first four paragraphs of "In the Zone" begin with a conjugation of tenses: "We are safely past . . ."; "They found the countryside, this year, at peace"; "Nordhausen puts less credence in the ice-saints . . ."; and "Signs will find him here in the Zone" (281).

These are modulations of Pynchon's voice. They alter our relationship to the "story" we are trying to follow, and are part of his strategy of keeping readers in an uncertain and active relation to his telling. The four sentences above alter our point of view, so that we are alternately "in" the story and "above" it. This is done without warning, as in the Kenosha Kid section (60–71) in which Slothrop's drug-induced hallucinations are conveyed through a fusion of first and third persons rather than a stream of con-sciousness: "He finds *he can* identify certain traces of shit. . . . Hey, here's that 'Gobbler' Biddle, must've been the night *we all ate* chop suey at Fu's Folly. . . . In its blunt, reluctant touches along the wall (which speak the reverse of its own cohesion) *he can*, uncannily shit-sensitized now, read old agonies" (italics mine, 65). Point of view here modulates from third person to first and back again to third, as the surface of the prose moves back and forth across the grammatical boundary separating the character in his world from the world of the narrator and reader.

This modulation is characteristic of the flowing, Orphic voice insisting on the impermanence of structures which appear to characters and readers as fixed. The intrusive voice in fiction usually serves the opposite purpose, as it does in Fielding and

Thackeray, who guide the reader and provide a fixed source of knowledge and value for the worlds in their books. Pynchon's voice retains the advantages of the intrusive, visible guide, but undermines the stability commonly associated with it, for his knowledge of the world of *Gravity's Rainbow* is fragmentary. He does know a good deal about the fragments he describes, however, and can move about among them at will, looking backward ("Once this happened," 303) and forward (Bloat is "too busy running through plausible excuses should he happen to get caught, not that he will, you know," 17) and providing through its persistence the coherence of an accompanying voice.

But there are gaps in Pynchon's omniscience, uncertainties and questions more than rhetorical (as is "What *can* young Osbie possibly have in mind?"): "A voice from some cell too distant for us to locate intones . . ." (231); "What did Tchitcherine have to say? Was Tchitcherine there at all?" (345); and "Wait—which one of them was thinking that? Monitors, get a fix on it, *hurry up*— But the target slips away" (298). A related example is Pynchon's decision not to tell us what happens to his characters. In the last chapter of *Tom Jones* Fielding writes, "As to the other persons who have made any considerable figure in this history, as some may desire to know a little more concerning them, we will proceed in as few words as possible, to satisfy their curiosity." The last chapter of *Vanity Fair* "contains births, marriages, and deaths." The Pequod sinks; Joyce's Stephen finds a home. By contrast, *Gravity's Rainbow* leaves Pirate in a tailspin, Katje with Enzian and the Hereros (do they send the rocket up?), Tchitcherine with Geli beside a stream (what happens to them?), Slothrop naked and alone in northern Germany, and we know Blicero will die but not how.

But this incompleteness is the result of the endless continuity of the world in process that Pynchon describes. *That* story cannot end, and what can be said about it is necessarily fragmentary. Pynchon's diffused, Orphic voice fills the world it describes instead of attempting to speak to us from a Jamesian vantage outside the world. The instability of the voice accords with the world it flows through, in constant change and transformation. The wild mustard in the center of the Autobahn down which Mexico drives is "perfectly two-tone, just yellow and green, a fateful river seen only by two kinds of rippling light" (627). The sun setting on London is an "incandescent sky casting downward across the miles of deep streets and roofs cluttering and sinuous river Thames a drastic stain of burnt orange to remind a visitor of his mortal transience here" (111–12). The factories and sheds of the Reinickendorf, into which Pokler wanders one night, are "expansions of brick into night and disuse" (160). Not "expanses" but "expansions": these walls are moving, decaying, and distorting right now, before us in the present tense of Pynchon's voice.

The present tense of *Gravity's Rainbow* is the essential characteristic of Pynchon's voice and the primary source of the uncertainty and transience which readers experience. It is more than the appropriate stance of an Orphic narrator, for the present tense emphasizes the tentative, conditional location of the "real present" of the reader. Pynchon's disposition is overwhelmingly for the present, but he will on occasion use other tenses for oratorical purposes. He has a peculiarly poignant way of throwing his story into the future and then picking it up again in the present, as in this example of the narrative transience being described here:

he will lunge after her without thinking much, slip himself as she vanishes under the chalky lifelines and gone, stagger trying to get back but be hit too soon in the kidneys and be flipped that easy over the side and it's adios to the *Anubis* and all its screaming Fascist cargo, already no more ship, not even black sky as the rain drives down his falling eyes now in quick needlestrokes, and he hits, without call for help, just a meek tearful *oh fuck*, tears that will add nothing to the whipped white desolation that passes for the Oder Haff tonight. . . . (491)

The Oder is a river that empties into the Baltic, but Pynchon adds "Haff," which is German for "freshwater lake connected with the sea," to enforce with that pun the fact that Tyrone has joined the ranks of the overlooked Preterite. The present tense reasserts itself at the same time that he loses his footing. What is past may seem clear, and the future does not yet impinge, but the present—like the Oder Haff—is the river in which Slothrop must swim. Pynchon's voice obscures all the distinctions in Tyrone's fall until there is only falling and falling water; ship and sky disappear, and even the river is but "whipped white desolation" only passing for the Oder Haff.

By far the most difficult consequence for readers "listening" to Pynchon's ever-present voice is the detachment of values which results. The flow of Pynchon's transformations not only dissolves the illusory stability of walls, characters, and plots but also makes it impossible for us to attach values to any of these forms within the book. The values Pynchon supports are clear in his elegy of loss, but they drift unattached to anything in the world he describes. Complicating this fact is Pynchon's evident distaste for any form of sentiment. Sentiment is feeling given form in memory, nostalgia, slogan, and other expressions; as such, for Pynchon, they immediately become part of the entire false accumulation which comprises and shapes our understanding. Pynchon's reluctance to provide a set of values that is consistently borne out by his fiction or as clearly denied is more than an act of technical virtuosity; it is a delicacy of heart, and an irony of love. The meticulous affection he shows for the objects of his attention stands in ironic opposition to the fragmented world he sees around himself.

Pynchon's unwillingness to attach his values to character or plot results in methods of indirection and ambiguity. The last time we see Benny Profane, he is with a college girl named Brenda Wigglesworth, who reads him a poem she's written. The poem begins, "I am the twentieth century," and continues in a vein which touches on all the major themes and images of the novel: "I am the Street, . . . the tourist-lady's hairpiece, . . . the traveling clock. . . . I am all the appurtenances of the night" (V., 428). Profane says " 'That sounds about right,' " and of course it is, but Brenda answers " 'It's a phony college-girl poem. Things I've read for courses.' " The courses have told her what the experience of the twentieth century means, but Brenda wants the direct experience to tell her something: " 'The experience, the experience. Haven't you learned?' " She's talking to the wrong character, for Profane has spent the entire novel avoiding learning anything from his experience. In the fine distinction drawn by Rachel Owlglass, Profane experiences life but does not live: " 'Once I will say it, is all: that Crew does not live, it experiences. It does not create, it talks about people who do' " (356).

The value of Pynchon's Orphic voice exists on that fine line between the phoniness of Brenda's borrowed understanding and the literal experience which carries no meaning. Pynchon wants to engage readers in the activity of meaning that exists between these two poles. Late in *Gravity's Rainbow* Seaman Bodine sings a song one night in the Chicago Bar. The drug merchants are "all dealing a bit slower. Sentimental Bodine thinks it's because they're listening to his song. Maybe they are" (740). Bodine is "sentimental" because he thinks they are listening to him; Pynchon is willing to say "maybe." In the Studentenheim Rebecca insists " 'there's coming together' " but Rudi, the narrative voice says, "turns away as we do from those who have just made some embarrassing appeal to faith there's no way to go into any further" (155). Pynchon is alert to the reactionary sentimentalism lurking in professions of faith and in any style which doesn't continue to question itself. Pynchon chides the Kenosha Kid, "There's nothing so loathsome as a sentimental surrealist" (696); yet the Kid's surrealism, after all, is Pynchon's. The censure is directed also at himself, which is a way of keeping the reader and the prose from slipping out of the present into a sure and distancing "understanding."

The result is that normative values in *Gravity's Rainbow* are left to fend for themselves. After listening to Enzian tell the story of his relationship with Weissmann, a companion summarizes, " 'Then ... what's happened, since your first days in Europe, could be described, in Max Weber's phrase, almost as a 'routinization of charisma.' " Enzian retorts, " 'Outase,' which is one of many Herero words for shit" (325). Enzian's answer does not mean that Weber's phrase is inapplicable, but the remark is itself a "routinization" of Enzian, to which he justly objects.

Values exist not in the world but in our ongoing relation to the world; they are the most transient of realities, depending for their existence upon the decision to affirm them in that relation. Values, therefore, exist not in single elements of *Gravity's Rainbow* but among the fragments and between the characters. The musical debate between the romantic Bummer and the atonalist Gustav is an instance of this. One night Säure insists:

"With Rossini, the whole point is that lovers always get together, isolation is overcome, and like it or not that is the one great centripetal movement of the World. Through the machineries of greed, pettiness, and the abuse of power, *love occurs*. All the shit is transmuted to gold.

The walls are breached, the balconies scaled—listen!" It was a night in early May, and the final bombardment of Berlin was in progress. Säure had to shout his head off. (440)

In this book values are always under bombardment, but they receive just enough support to prevent their complete disintegration. And the effect of the above passage is not desolation but laughter. Gustav's response is just as funny and equally persuasive: "'They're all listening to Rossini! Sitting there drooling away to some medley of predictable little tunes, leaning forward elbows on knees muttering, "C'mon, c'mon then Rossini, let's get all this pretentious fanfare stuff out of the way, let's get on to the *real good tunes!*"'" (441). Both of them survive the shelling and this is not the end of their debate.[26] In one of its later stages Säure erupts, "'*Sound* is a game, if you're capable of moving that far, you adenoidal closet-visionary. That's why I listen to Spohr, Rossini, Spontini, I'm choosing *my* game, one full of light and kindness. You're stuck with that stratosphere stuff and rationalize its dullness away by calling it "enlightenment." You don't know what enlightenment is, Kerl, you're blinder than I am'" (622). Säure's argument gains support here by its reference to Weber, and his recognition that Rossini's music is not truth but represents the values he would rather promote.

But this debate is just one of thousands of fragments which make up *Gravity's Rainbow*. Säure's values are chosen, not fixed, and they compete with hundreds of other dogmas, systems, and aspirations in the book. Säure's kindness, Geli's love, and the mercy-spared Ilse have to confront Mexico's loss, Slothrop's disassembly, and Pointsman's ambition. Each of these elements presents itself to the reader as a possible final understanding of *Gravity's Rainbow*, but no one of them is elevated to that status. The book remains as unresolved as the world of competing values in which we live.

Pynchon's voice further frustrates the reader's attempt to find a stable world of values by giving readers no one to hate. Thackeray never lets his readers forget that Rebecca Sharp is a bad woman. Though he is a master at showing the vixen's deceitfulness, he reserves the right to tell us what he thinks about his characters: "if they are good and kindly, to love them and shake them by the hand; if they are silly, to laugh at them confidentially in the reader's sleeve; if they are wicked and heartless, to abuse them in the strongest terms which politeness admits of."[27] The characters of *Gravity's Rainbow* are given too much human detail, we know too much about their fears, ambitions, and dreams, for us to dismiss such figures as Pointsman and Weissmann. The less-developed figures such as Mossmoon and Scammony are easily scorned, but they occupy so little space in the book that this unambiguous emotion gives no foothold, and hardly counts beside the disturbing empathy evoked for the other well-developed characters. Enzian's understanding and love of Blicero mitigates and questions what disgust we may feel for Weissmann. Katje's role in the Pointsman plot is softened by her affection for Tyrone and by her defection to the Counterforce which goes looking for him. Pointsman himself possesses a tragic humanness in the completeness with which his hopes are shown; he is loved briefly by Maudie Chilkes (tropics do touch his Pavlovian winter), he is capable of writing Wordsworthian "excursions," and he ends feeling "sentimental over a pack of slobbering curs" (752). Rejected and passed over, Pointsman becomes one of us, a member of the Preterite.

If anything is stable in *Gravity's Rainbow*, it is this insistence upon the humility of the Preterite lost in the labyrinthine confusion of a world where the stability of simple distinctions is absent. The intimacy which develops between Pynchon's voice and his listeners is not the cozy, smug conspiracy that Thackeray invites, because Pynchon's song implicates us all in the fragmentation we share. There is in this a tremendous communal impulse, as Pynchon urges us: "listen to this mock-angel singing, let your communion be at least in listening, even if they are not spokesmen for your exact hopes" (135). Pynchon has always addressed his isolated readers as sharing a preterition, feebs and tankers, glozing neuters all, a community he shares by his palpable absence. By the end of *Gravity's Rainbow* the last "Now, everybody—" which first we heard, distant, years ago in the London mime show with Roger and Jessica—is extended to us, the last survivors in Pynchon's Orpheus Theatre, where his fragmented voice asks us to join in the communion of his difficult song.

NOTES

1. *Introduction to Aristotle*, ed. Richard McKeon (New York: Modern Library, 1947), p. 637. The passage is from chapter nine of *De Poetica*.
2. *The Sacred and the Profane* (New York: Harcourt, Brace & World, 1959), p. 11 and throughout. Please note that Edward Mendelson traces Pynchon's use of this word to Eliade in his study of *The Crying of Lot 49*, cited earlier. I expressed my reservations about Mendelson's conclusions in "Open Letter in Response to Edward Mendelson's 'The Sacred, the Profane and *The Crying of Lot 49*'" *Boundary 2*, 5 (Fall, 1976), 93–101.
3. See especially chapter 2, pp. 24–40, of *The Fantastic*, trans. Richard Howard (Cleveland: Press of Case Western Reserve University, 1973).
4. *Sacred*, p. 12.
5. For this piece of detective serendipity I have Dr. James McBride to thank, a professor of mathematical statistics, who told me that the V-bomb example is commonly used in textbooks and suggested Feller. Since then, Khachig Tölölyan has presented a brief and persuasive argument that the statistics text Pynchon actually used was Yule and Kendall's *An Introduction to the Theory of Statistics*. Tölölyan's article, "The Fishy Poisson: Allusions to Statistics in *Gravity's Rainbow*," appears in *Notes on Modern American Literature*, 4, no. 1 (1979).
6. Vol. 72 (1944–46), 481.
7. William Feller, *An Introduction to Probability Theory and Its Applications*, 1 (New York: John Wiley, 1957), 152.
8. The mathematical form of the Poisson distribution is

$$p(k;\lambda) = e^{-\lambda}\,\frac{\lambda^k}{k!}$$

And Feller's explanation: "The physical assumptions which we want to express mathematically are that the conditions of the experiment remain constant in time, and that non-overlapping time intervals are stochastically independent in the sense that information concerning the number of events in one interval reveals nothing about the other" (pp. 146–47). This is what Mexico means when he says to Pointsman: "Bombs are not dogs. No link. No memory. No conditioning" (*GR*, 56).
9. See "Nosepicking Contests," *Time*, 87 (May 6, 1966), 109–10.
10. See, for example, Paul Fussell, *The Great War and Modern Memory* (New York: Oxford University Press, 1975), p. 328. There are also several books published about the Special Operations Executive.
11. (Chicago: Chicago Literary Club, 1938), p. 13.
12. *Ibid.*, pp. 13–19.

13. *Ibid.*, p. 26.
14. There are, for example, many reasons why the moon as the female "underground" presence congruent with the daytime sun should be used by Pynchon as part of the imagery of *The Crying of Lot 49;* the moon is associated with the community of exile, since the Pacific is "the hole left by the moon's tearing-free and monument to her exile" (*CL49*, 37). But consider the fact that, according to the Columbia Encyclopedia, the volume of the moon is "very nearly *one forty-ninth* that of the earth."
15. "The New Vision of Science," *Harper's Magazine*, 158 (March, 1929), 451.
16. See "The ABC of ESP," in *The Roots of Coincidence* (New York: Random House, 1972).
17. This fact occasions the apologetic tone one finds in Pynchon criticism. That Pynchon's writing engenders such hesitation is a sign of its strength. Two excellent discussions of this may be found in Richard Poirier's "The Importance of Thomas Pynchon" in *Mindful Pleasures*, ed. Levine and Leverenz, pp. 15–29 and Mendelson's introduction to *Pynchon: A Collection of Critical Essays.*
18. William P. Trent, *A History of American Literature, 1607–1865* (New York: D. Appleton, 1903), p. 390.
19. (New York: Harper & Row, 1971).
20. *Ibid.*, pp. 129–30.
21. *The Ascent of Man* (Boston: Little, Brown, 1973), p. 340.
22. *Van Nostrand's Scientific Encyclopedia* (New York: D. Van Nostrand, 1947).
23. See the chapter by that title in Otto Friedrich's *Before the Deluge: A Portrait of Berlin in the 1920's* (New York: Harper & Row, 1972), pp. 212–40.
24. This is one of many allusions in *Gravity's Rainbow* to Ralph Ellison's *Invisible Man.*
25. Pynchon's place in the Puritan rhetorical tradition is discussed in an essay by Marcus Smith and Khachig Tölölyan, "*Gravity's Rainbow* and the Puritan Jeremiad," in *Critical Articles on Thomas Pynchon*, ed. Richard Pearce (Boston: G. K. Hall, 1980).
26. Read Friedrich's discussion of Schoenberg's battle against the traditional system of tonality, in *Before the Deluge*, "The Supremacy of German Music," pp. 167–88.
27. *Vanity Fair*, Riverside Edition (Boston: Houghton Mifflin, 1963), p. 81.

Six

Pynchon's Company

Ad Hoc Fiction and the Politics of Experience

> "I go to encounter for the millionth time the reality of experience and to forge in the smithy of my soul the uncreated conscience of my race."
> James Joyce, *A Portrait of the Artist as a Young Man*

> *Teach them that anywhere people go they have experience and that all experience is art.*
> Ishmael Reed, *Yellow Back Radio Broke-Down*

Before concluding this essay on Thomas Pynchon, some account should be given of the social significance of the glib, slapstick, comic-book aspects of his writing which cause consternation among some readers. I have already suggested that one reason for the brilliant surfaces of Pynchon's narratives is the direction they take toward simultaneous meaning and their movement away from "one-way" history and personal psychology. The surfaces of his fiction have depth but remain impenetrable. I hope I have also indicated Pynchon's uncanny ability to summon historical detail and evoke personal feeling where it suits his purposes.

There is, however, another and equally important reason for this aspect of Pynchon's writing, which, in turn, helps to define the writers I call *Pynchon's company*. This company includes contemporary writers who pretend, for serious reasons, not to be serious. These writers present social and psychological views which have dramatic political consequences, but they do so without the seriousness and romantic self-importance of such modernist writers as Eliot and Joyce. The fiction of such writers as Richard Fariña, M. F. Beal (Mary Shetzline), Tom Robbins,

Peter Matthiessen, Ishmael Reed, and William S. Burroughs has arisen in part as a literary development of the democracy of experience associated with the period of Viet Nam protest, the black movement of the last thirty years, and the resurgence of feminism. These specific historical events are only the most visible examples of a broad diffusion of the idea that each person's experience is the equal of another's and that all experience may be the subject of art.

The affirmation of variety is always political. The writing of Pynchon's company is an ad hoc opposition to the recurring tendencies of a culture to establish some experiences as more valuable and significant than others. Some experiences *are* more valuable than others, but the established preferences of a culture—those experiences which a culture celebrates and encourages its members to desire—are in covert league with the political and economic systems that fostered desire supports. The modernists in the early years of this century opposed such an established hierarchy of experience; the vision, satire, and parody of Pynchon's company is part of the revaluation of culture and literary subject matter that is a recurrent fact of literary history.

The writers I refer to are not, I think, comparable in stature to Thomas Pynchon. They lack his versatility, his rhetorical power, and his complexity (that is to say, adequacy) of understanding. Even where they do share social, philosophical, and political ideas with him, they do not dramatize these ideas with anything approaching the entangling ambiguity in which Pynchon's writing involves readers. Nonetheless, these writers—including Pynchon—are committed to a fiction of social fantasy which in varying ways and degrees is revolutionary and enlivening, social and energizing. Their writing represents an expression of opposition whose value lies not so much in any literal alternative their fiction offers as in the charisma of its opposition, and in the paranoid energies of its existence as a kind of renegade fiction. By grouping these writers together, I do not mean to blur the distinctiveness of each, but to point to underlying impulses common to all of them. For them writing is the creation and flaunting of freedom in the face of a systematic seriousness which dismisses humane alternatives, threatens the planet, and incarcerates entire dimensions of experience in the categories of the "trivial" and "illegal."

In his jacket blurb for Fariña's *Been Down So Long It Looks Like Up to Me,* Pynchon describes the book as coming "on like the Hallelujah Chorus done by 200 kazoo players with perfect pitch, I mean strong, swinging, skillful and reverent—but also with the fine brassy buzz of irreverence in there too. Fariña has going for him an unerring and virtuoso instinct about exactly what, in this bewildering Republic, is serious and what cannot possibly be."[1] The comment may be taken as a partial esthetic of Pynchon's company; it amounts to a code that forbids the writer from becoming lost in a sentimental (and self-serving) reverence for tradition. The dissonance and joy of imagining kazoos in perfect pitch is especially characteristic of Pynchon's intentions, since opposition in his writing is always convoluted and embodied in discordant wholes. For others of the company, whose goals more nearly resemble the allegories of morality plays, the opposition between tradition and irreverence may fall neatly into opposing characters, as they do in *Yellow Back Radio Broke-Down.*

Irreverence is always a critique, not only of what has been designated "sacred" and "true" but also of the entrenched power that enforces such designations. Pynchon's casual reference to the nonexistent "Vivaldi Kazoo Concerto" in the midst of an otherwise plausible and satiric list of Oedipa's housewifely chores is a comic jab whose sharpness depends upon the degree and nature of our respect for Vivaldi. Pynchon's references to classical pieces for the kazoo (see "the suppressed quartet from the Haydn Op. 76, the so-called 'Kazoo Quartet' in G-Flat Minor" in *Gravity's Rainbow,* p. 711) contribute to his satire of the established white traditions, in this case of western music, from which kazoos and other instruments of the Preterite have been excluded. That Pynchon asks us to think of classical composers and kazoos together is an essential feature of his humor, which, deadpan, assumes that the unlikely is plausible. Tyrone, the mock Orpheus of *Gravity's Rainbow,* plays the harmonica, not the lyre.

Kazoos are part of the paraphernalia of the opposition, which includes Robbins's cowgirls, Reed's circus of children, the "Lindy" of Malcolm X, exploding cigars, bright colors, tasteless jokes, and whatever is neglected, discarded, and suppressed. Thus, when

Tyrone suspects, in the game room of the Casino Goering, that "there is another enterprise here," he responds as one of the Preterite: "'Fuck you,' whispers Slothrop. It's the only spell he knows, and a pretty good all-purpose one at that. His whisper is baffled by the thousands of tiny rococo surfaces. Maybe he'll sneak in tonight—no not at night—but sometime, with a bucket and brush, paint FUCK YOU in a balloon coming out the mouth of one of those little pink shepherdesses there . . ." (203). Though Tyrone's response is lonely and ineffectual, it is related to the more convivial exploits of the Counterforce later in the book. Pynchon's floundering rebels are relatives of Reed's Loop Garoo Kid and the children of Yellow Back Radio, and of Tom Robbins's cowgirls, who repulse the squeamish, male Countess by stripping naked from the waist down.

These satiric exaggerations are an expression of outrage against a culture which has habitually sought control over the world and the world's manifold variety. The writing of Pynchon's company exists as a kind of literary drug seeking to alter the consciousness of the reader for the purpose of altering social and political structures which inhibit, narrow, and reduce what we are allowed to think of as "real" and "important."[2] As "highbrow" culture displays its power by a preference for tasteful and refined colors of subtle shade and hue, so must Pynchon's company celebrate comic-book colors accessible to all, which delight children and announce circuses. Seaman ("Pig") Bodine arrives at the Utgarthaloki dinner party dressed in a *"paint*-blue" zoot suit; Tyrone wears a gaudy Hawaiian shirt to fight the gray Grigori. By contrast, the plastic shroud which Zhlubb fears will choke him is white (756), an echo of Gottfried's Imipolex shroud, described two pages previously as "gray-white, mocking, an enemy of color" (754).

The appearance of "Sunday funnies" irreverence in our serious reading is part of a conscious intention on the part of these writers to offset the "absence of surprise to life" (*CL49*, 128). Surprise is germane to comic effect and is an affirmative response to adversity and the imminence of death. Comedy dwells on the ways in which life stubbornly persists and unexpectedly continues. Clown after clown jumps from the tiny car; is it possible that

Vivaldi really wrote a kazoo concerto? Whenever we are surprised it seems there is again the possibility that the world may never be used up.

Pynchon's company provides improbabilities in a culture addicted to the probable, and to the control which predictability permits. This is Tom Robbins's analysis of the pleasure we take in UFO sightings: "Would you not, sooner or later, no matter who or what you are, feel a rise in spirit, a kind of wild-card joy as a result of your encounter? And if this elevation, this joyousness, can be attributed in part to your contact with . . . Mystery . . . cannot it equally be attributed to your abrupt realization that there are superior forces 'out there,' forces that for all their potential menace, nevertheless might, should they elect to intervene, represent salvation for a planet that seems stubbornly determined to perish?"[3] This fearful elation is Robbins's version of Pynchon's "*singularities*," which carry a "luminosity and enigma at which something in us must leap and sing, or withdraw in fright" (*GR*, 396).

The appearance of surprise in fiction has many motives, but in the current writing I am discussing here its underlying impulse is a reaction to the direction our culture has taken. Members of the company are outraged, and their work often modulates into forms akin to lecture and essay, as in Pynchon's marvelous pages on Kekulé's dream (*GR*, 410–13). Burroughs's disjointed *Naked Lunch* is a purposeful neglect of continuity, requiring readers to confront his junkie vision nakedly, without the ease and control of an imposed understanding. This method conforms to Burroughs's criticism of American culture: "Americans have a special horror of giving up control, of letting things happen in their own way without interference. They would like to jump down into their stomachs and digest the food and shovel the shit out."[4] Burroughs's book, intelligible and consistent on the level of its meanings, obeys the "one-thing-leads-to-another" movement of mind which characterizes Robbins's heroine Sissy Hankshaw.[5]

The battle between control and surprise is the recurring drama in Pynchon's company. It appears in Ishmael Reed's *Mumbo Jumbo* as the conflict between Set—"the 1st man to shut nature out of himself. He called it discipline"—and his brother Osiris—dancer, "adept at the mysteries of agriculture."[6] In *Mumbo*

Jumbo, Reed suddenly abandons his story to present this revision of "mytho-cultural history,"[7] in which the Egyptian god Osiris is revealed to have been black, and Sir James Frazer's Victorian view of fertility rites is rewritten as a celebration of "the processes of blooming."[8] Reed's purposes allow him to distinguish simply between the "uptight" and the loose, between the taxman and the dancer. For Pynchon, these oppositions exist congruent with one another, as is hinted by "the soft dusk of mirrors" in Oedipa's dreams. Tyrone's dream definition of Lazlo Jamf as himself twists opposition into an unsettling ambiguity. White Tyrone is the "Schwarzknabe," the black child fearful of blackness, shit, and death (*GR*, 285–87, 623). Pynchon incorporates *The Autobiography of Malcolm X* into the story of Tyrone (62–65, 688) not only to aid in uncovering Slothrop's representative fears, but also because Malcolm's written story is a political example of the importance of an alternative black history and myth which counters the paleface mythology of the American Western, Lone-Rangerism, and Heart-of-Darkness imperialism. Slothrop's trip down the toilet is the beginning of an education in his own blackness. By the end of *Gravity's Rainbow*, the harmonica, Tyrone's "silver chances of song," has become symbolic of the scattered mock Orpheus and the hapless opponents of those forces who have institutionalized the original Orphic singers. Zhlubb, manager of the Orpheus Theatre, like Reed's Set, "has come out against what he calls 'irresponsible use of the harmonica'" (*GR*, 754).

For many writers of Pynchon's company, the battle is simply that between the vicious "brain game" called "rational thought"[9] and blooming, unpredictable, spontaneous life. Rationality, the ordering of thoughts, and bureaucratic system are artificial structures imposed upon what would otherwise be natural and instinctive. If only we would leave the universe (including ourselves) alone—this is how the thinking goes—the universe would operate as automatically as the stomach's digestion. There is implied in the fiction of many of these writers—and here they part company with Pynchon—a latent normalcy full of sentience and vitality which could be ours if we would but *relax*. Near the end of *Yellow Back Radio Broke-Down*, the villain Drag has almost run out of tricks when the children arrive in a Chicken Delight truck announcing they have found the Seven Cities of Cibola. Drag revives: "If there's some kind of Cibola place what's got exploitive possibilities I'm going to be the one to get the coin." The children answer: "Aw come off it Drag . . . act normal will ya?"[10]

All of the company insist upon a living universe of variety and beauty, threatened but surviving, whose forms of life are as important as we are. This is the most affirmative and releasing element of their writing, for the possibility that life might exist in other time frames, be calibrated in other frequencies, and visible in lights hidden from us is both an affirmation of life's variety and a vantage from which our lives no longer seem "exitless." No one of these writers more than Peter Matthiessen—whose writing is without satire or slapstick—has given such emphasis to the vitality of the natural world and our relation to it. Lewis Moon, the protagonist of *At Play in the Fields of the Lord*, moves between the opposed and stock characters of the white missionary and the noble savage to a savannah beyond the rain forest and an "exultant" place in Nature: "Laid naked to the sun and sky, he felt himself open like a flower. Soon he slept. At dark he built an enormous fire, in celebration of the only man beneath the eye of Heaven."[11]

The story of Lewis Moon provides a helpful parallel to the story of Slothrop, who, like Moon, journeys through the world until he stands naked beneath the sky. The meaning of Tyrone's experience, however, remains more ambiguous than Moon's clear exultation. Throughout the novel, Moon has been a conventionally realistic character. In his final scene, Moon retains his consciousness and celebrates himself, his clean nakedness, and his nameless unencumbered being. Tyrone's release from the trials of identity is won at the cost of his scattering in the world and the fragmentation of the novel, which persists. Whether this is a kind of success is never clear. The difference in the two similar endings (of the characters' existences) points up the fact that Pynchon's book is more elegiac and satiric than Matthiessen's, whose work indicates a truly visionary resolution of contradictions that remain inseparable and dissonant in Pynchon's writing. Lying beneath the work of both, however, is the shared belief in the sentience of the natural world and the necessity of its preservation.

While all of these writers differ in emphasis, manner, and mood, collectively they are part of a literary resistance to the forces of constriction and denial. Their opposing voice is an enormously enjoyable and healthy element in current writing. What these writers are intent on publishing is important, and while an overt preoccupation with theme may at times produce indifferent writing which is more instructive than pleasing, it is instruction to which we can ill afford to be indifferent.

An American Tradition

> Thus, therefore, the floor of our familiar room has become a neutral territory, somewhere between the real world and fairy-land, where the Actual and the Imaginary may meet, and each imbue itself with the nature of the other.
>
> Nathaniel Hawthorne, "The Custom House"

> For, in certain moods, no man can weigh this world, without throwing in something, somehow like Original Sin, to strike the uneven balance.
>
> Herman Melville, "Hawthorne and His Mosses"

Pynchon's ambiguities belong to the literary heritage in the American tradition represented by Hawthorne and Melville. Pynchon's work belongs with those American narratives which recognize and enact the dark underside "invisible yet congruent with the cheered land" (CL49, 135). The narrative fiction of this tradition incorporates the entropic tendencies which have—even before its inception—shared in the composition of our republic's image, reflecting the fact that American culture—its promise preconceived and ideal—has always fallen short of the spiritual meaning which the early settlers imagined for the land.[12] The inherent contradiction between ideal and material reality remains an unresolved drama in the evolution of American society, one which accounts in part for the tendency of American writers to explore "the aesthetic possibilities of radical forms of alienation, contradiction and disorder."[13]

In this tradition promise is congruent with decline, and "education" always means instruction in the poverty, decay, and death which the bright surfaces of America deny. At this point in the tradition, such an education is a self-conscious portion of the American inheritance, and Pynchon is able to portray Oedipa and Tyrone in terms that evoke this persistent theme, now familiar to us all: "The one ghost-feather his fingers always brush by is America. Poor asshole, he can't let her go. She's whispered *love me* too often to him in his sleep, vamped insatiably his waking attention with come-hitherings, incredible promises" (*GR*, 623).

This theme is visibly autobiographical, since for these writers their work is the necessary demonstration of a separateness from the more public, commercial drives of the culture. They are like Oedipa: "The only way she could continue, and manage to be at all relevant to [America], was as an alien" (*CL49*, 137). The lives and documents of Poe, Hawthorne, Melville, James, Twain, Faulkner, Ellison—to further sketch the line—are studies in the difficulty they faced in relating to America. That difficulty appears in their writing as the precarious middle ground their characters inhabit. Ishmael and Hester must absorb and admit conflicting meanings that are kept whole only in the imaginative use of the symbols central to their stories. The personal guilt which goes with the territory of alienation expresses a social contradiction unfelt by Jason Compson and Flem Snopes, who represent but one side of the conflict. The typical protagonists—Hester, Ishmael, Huck, Quentin, Oedipa—must endure both sides of the American polarity, for they are inevitably returned to the fact of their complicity in what they inherit, in what follows them, in what they create, wherever they go.

Pynchon recaptures the continuing importance of this American heritage, but his fiction is international in scope and criticizes a western culture of which America is the most recent and virulent example. " 'One would have to exorcise . . . the continents, the world. Or the western part,' " Maijstral tells Sidney Stencil. " 'We are western men' " (*V.*, 424). The setting for *Gravity's Rainbow* is therefore appropriate for at least two reasons: literally, after World War II American culture metastasized throughout the world, and figuratively, Tyrone's disappearance in northern Europe is not only an alienation from America but from the western origins of our republic. Pynchon places America at the furthest edge of "Western man's" colonizing of the world. His writing integrates Conrad's view of civilization as a white force mining the southern darkness, trying in this way to domesticate the black unknown which threatens our conscious lives. In *Gravity's Rainbow*, this push returns on Europe with its deathly rationalism and remakes the postwar world in its own image: "Now we are in the last phase. American Death has come to occupy Europe. It has learned empire from its old metropolis" (*GR*, 722). By means of the book's allusions to Richard Nixon, *Gravity's Rainbow* moves forward to the late 1960s and the moon landing, which Weissmann foresees as the base camp of man's stellar exploration and colonizing. From Europe to America and back again, to the world and the moon and beyond, "this is not a disentanglement from, but a progressive *knotting* into" (*GR*, 3).

We know little more of Thomas Pynchon's biography than his family lineage,[14] but this is sufficient to indicate the importance for Pynchon of Slothrop's story and to confirm an autobiographical relation between his own Orphic voice and Tyrone's disassembly. Pynchon's family history represents a colonizing strain that was overwhelmed by the cartelization of the world it helped to propagate. The minds and spirits which colonized America have been lost in the reification of power structures which they brought into being, and which are now as permanent and invisible as the spirit of enterprise itself. From this vantage, Tyrone's loss of identity is the peculiar American loss of its dream-identity; distaste for what that dream has become dismembers his "recklessness transatlantic" (182). The dream of what could be is replaced by the Orphic song of what has been.

This autobiographical aspect of *Gravity's Rainbow* underlines Pynchon's realism of relation, his mimesis of the effort to establish a relation to America and the culture of the world. The "trans-observable" oddities of his fiction are those of a mind trying to remain whole. The involutions of *V.*, *The Crying of Lot 49*, and *Gravity's Rainbow* are not truly psychological, but are social twistings of the sort Mucho Maas discerns in the ceaseless exchange of used cars he oversees: "To Mucho it was horrible. Endless, convoluted incest" (*CL49*, 5). In this extended, social sense, Pynchon's books are documentaries of social incest. Oedipa's discoveries are convoluted because they must be, because she herself—first in her suburban life and then in her scholarly gumshoeing—is representative of the ordering impulses which perpetuate and afflict her society, just as Oedipus's crime is the origin of his own society's plague.

The convolutions of Pynchon's writing, according to some readers, ally Pynchon with another group of contemporary writers whose primary interest is the fictiveness of fiction. Like Pynchon's company, this group is impatient with the unreality of "realism" and is distrustful of the rational mind. Their response, however, is inward toward the Cartesian cogito, rather than outward, to "reality" and community. Their fiction is about writing and perception; the connection between self and world is absent in the extreme examples of their work. Pynchon's mirror-hauntings should not be confused with, for example, the self-referentiality of John Barth's later fiction. For Pynchon's authorial intrusions are the vigorous outpourings of a mind keenly aware of the mind's role in social and political reality.

In our time the labyrinth of the mind has become the scapegoat of modern confusion. We see this expressed in the plotted mazes of John Fowles's character Conchis in *The Magus*, and in Barth's Ambrose. The latter becomes lost in the funhouse because he tries to understand its reflections. By contrast, Pynchon's books depend upon the animating power and inevitability of thinking; at the same time they are cautions against the tendency of thinking to become formal doctrine. Such stories as Barth's "Title" and Robert Coover's "The Babysitter" have ramifications which reach feeling through thought, but these fictions are wholly "made." These stories are about being themselves, and their significance for social and political history is secondary. In its extreme form this fiction has as its subject the infinite regress of mind, of cerebration without traction, as in Barth's "Autobiography": "my last words will be my last words."[15] This writing points to the interior perplexities of writing, not out, to the society at large: "Oh god comma I abhor self-consciousness. I despise what I have come to; I loathe our loathsome loathing."[16]

For Pynchon the conundrums of language and perception are constraints within the world. These conundrums supply some of the material of his writing, but they do not limit his subjects and they are not his central concern. It is customary to argue, as Charles Russell does, that "contemporary fiction is grounded in the recognition that all human meaning is asserted in the face of an apparently indifferent universe." Current writers, he continues, use language with the knowledge that "all linguistic systems are fundamentally arbitrary," and that "ultimately, meaning can refer only to its own linguistic system. It has only a self-referential significance." He groups Pynchon with Kosinski, Sukenick, and Barthelme, all of whom write fiction that "emphasizes the epistemological dimension of the artwork. . . . It offers not a study of the world, but of how experience is filtered through consciousness."[17]

Pynchon's writing includes *both* a "study of the world" and an examination of "how experience is filtered through consciousness." In fact, this is not a distinction that makes much sense in discussing Pynchon's fiction, where dreams, fears, and ambitions percolate through events more visible and concrete than they. The distinction assumed in the idea of a discrete self observing a discrete world is dissolved in Pynchon's writing. Inside and outside are merged, not in solipsism but in the totality of connectedness. There are many examples of this connectedness in Pynchon's writing. Some are concisely stated, as in this description of Major Marvy's encounter with the Iron Toad and Mother Ground: ". . . the great, the planetary pool of electrons making you one with your prototype" (604). Of course, epistemological questions threaten Stencil, Oedipa, and Tyrone—they are among the symmetrical possibilities which confront them—but their searches discover an actual social and political history the existence of which Pynchon's books never question. The Hereros were slaughtered; so were the Kazakhs. Language may be used to say these things, and still serves the communal purpose of providing a linguistic bond among people.

Pynchon's books are not self-reflexive because they reveal and document the reality of history. He acknowledges the paradoxes of language but retains the social power of the naturalistic novel. In Pynchon's writing language succeeds in binding people together. Tchitcherine's father manages a few days off ship with a Herero girl, and by "the time he left, they had learned each other's names and a few words in the respective languages—afraid, happy, sleep, love . . . the beginnings of a new tongue, a pidgin which they were perhaps the only two speakers of in the world" (*GR*, 351).

This small anecdote in Vaslav's history is part of the Kirghiz Light episode that contains much of what Pynchon has to say about language.[18] Throughout the book, language and light are allied, common magic against silence and darkness. Almost every section of "Beyond the Zero" includes an image of mankind (in London, the Kalihari, Germany) huddled around a form of light (sensitive's flame, flashlight, autoclave, cigarette ash, campfire, rocket exhaust, village meeting), speaking words and seeking the power of illumination against darkness, of song against the roar of silence.

The Kirghiz Light, however, is light of a different order. Like all intimations of revelation in Pynchon, it preserves its allure by remaining withheld. Both human language and mortal light are insufficient magic, but both are a source of meaningfulness among people. Tchitcherine and sidekick Džaqyp Qulan, in search of the Kirghiz Light, ride into the midst of a Kazakh singing-duel. The village people are gathered around the singers, a boy and a girl, forming a mandala. This particular duel becomes strident, but the wise aqyn seemingly dozing nearby "radiates for the singers a sort of guidance" that turns a "village apocalypse" into "comic cooperation." The aqyn's poetic response to Tchitcherine distinguishes two uses of language:

> If words were known, and spoken,
> Then the God might be a gold ikon,
> Or a page in a paper book.
> But It comes as the Kirghiz Light—
> There is no other way to know It.

The distinction escapes Tchitcherine, who has taken the words down in stenography (356–59). Behind this irony is the historical fact that the New Turkic Alphabet has destroyed the oral culture: "So the magic that the shamans, out in the wind, have always known, begins to operate now in a political way, and Džaqyp Qulan hears the ghost of his own lynched father with a scratchy pen in the night, practicing As and Bs . . ." (356). Such subject matter is profoundly social. Pynchon's Kirghiz episode dramatizes language as a force in the world and not as a limit of our being.

By insisting upon the power of language in the world, Pynchon's writing helps preserve a critical distance between private thought and public vision. His writing keeps us in an uncertain but engaged equilibrium between the extremes of self and society. This is the reason he is the most compelling social writer we have. The complexity of his understanding prevents opposition from declining into false division. His fiction reminds us of what a true society would mean, and articulates a society of isolation that already exists.[19] The paradox of Pynchon's career thus far is that a writer so vehemently communal should be so resolutely private; but this is only a seeming paradox, for publicity is not community and exchanges being known well for being well known.

It is in his isolation that Pynchon remains one of us. His perfect absence from the public view contributes to the scattered presence of his Orphic voice. His absence gives his books a curious autonomy they would not otherwise possess and assists them in blurring the readerly distinction between fiction and the real world. His disembodied voice gives vitality and importance to the neglected and private details of the life beyond his fiction. His writing therefore keeps us company and awakens in us the possibility that we are not alone. This awakening is the "physical grace" of Thomas Pynchon, at once communal and incomplete, a continuity of song that never resolves. Listen.

NOTES

1. (New York: Random House, 1966). *Gravity's Rainbow* is dedicated to Richard Fariña.

2. Consider, for example, this passage from M. F. Beal's *Amazon One*, a neo-journalist account of Weatherman activities: "You might be

shaking, with the heavy drum bursting in your chest, but it kept you *knowing* what was at stake: which was of course not to face them, that was not your job at all, but rather to hold the line somewhere against that type of craziness which saw the future as a well-oiled machine soldier-anting the universe" (Boston: Little, Brown, 1975), p. 5. The thinker in this passage is part of a plan to blow up the Bank of America in Berkeley, California. Pynchon's support of the book appeared in an advertisement for *Amazon One* in the *New York Times Book Review*, Apr. 13, 1975, p. 31. Pynchon mentions M. F. Beal in *Gravity's Rainbow* (p. 612).

3. *Even Cowgirls Get the Blues* (Boston: Houghton-Mifflin, 1976), p. 50. Inside the cover of the paperback edition of Robbins's book, Pynchon calls it a "piece of working magic, warm, funny, and sane" and hopes it will change "the brainscape of America." His phrase "working magic" is another expression of "Pig" Bodine's "physical grace" (*GR*, 741).

4. William S. Burroughs, *Naked Lunch* (New York: Grove Press, 1959), p. 215.

5. Robbins, *Cowgirls*, p. 116.

6. (Garden City, N.Y.: Doubleday, 1972), p. 162. In Pynchon's story of Lyle Bland, he refers us to Reed's *Mumbo Jumbo:* "Keep in mind where those Masonic Mysteries came from in the first place. (Check out Ishmael Reed. He knows more about it than you'll ever find here.)" (p. 588).

7. For this phrase, and help in clarifying my thinking about Reed, I thank Jeff Bartlett.

8. Reed, *Mumbo Jumbo*, p. 161.

9. Robbins, *Cowgirls*, p. 116.

10. Reed, *Yellow Back Radio Broke-Down* (New York: Avon Books, 1969), p. 205.

11. Peter Matthiessen, *At Play in the Fields of the Lord* (New York: Random House, 1965), p. 373. Pynchon expressed his admiration of Matthiessen's work on the back cover of the Bantam edition of *Far Tortuga:* "I've enjoyed everything I've ever read by Matthiessen, and this novel is Matthiessen at his best—a masterfully spun yarn, a little other-worldly, a dreamlike momentum.... Like everything else of his, it's also a deep declaration of love for the planet."

12. This view of American origins is discussed wonderfully in the first two chapters of Howard Mumford Jones's *O Strange New World* (New York: Viking Press, 1964).

13. Richard Chase, *The American Novel and Its Tradition* (Garden City, N.Y.: Doubleday, 1957), p. 2. My brief comments assume a familiarity with the ideas in Chase's book, especially the opening chapter, "The Broken Circuit," pp. 1–28. My purpose in these pages is to suggest ways in which Pynchon is contributing to the tradition of American narrative, and to use that tradition to further our under-

standing of Pynchon. Along these lines, Leslie Fiedler's analysis of the intentions of Melville and Hawthorne is useful: "For tragic Humanists, it is the function of art not to console or sustain, much less to entertain, but to *disturb* by telling a truth which is always unwelcome." *Love and Death in the American Novel* (New York: Stein & Day, 1966), p. 432.

14. See Mathew Winston's "The Quest for Pynchon."

15. *Lost in the Funhouse* (Garden City, N.Y.: Doubleday, 1968), p. 39. Barth's work, of course, is extremely varied. I refer to this example of his writing because it is representative of the self-conscious and baroque fiction of "exhaustion." He revises the views of his earlier essay in his discussion of "postmodernist fiction," titled "The Literature of Replenishment" *The Atlantic*, 245, no. 1 (January, 1980), 65–71.

16. *Ibid.*, p. 113.

17. "The Vault of Language: Self-Reflective Artifice in Contemporary American Fiction," *Modern Fiction Studies*, 20, no. 3 (Autumn, 1974), 351–52. Literary criticism has been dominated in recent years by a fascination with what Barth has called "French hyperbole." One of the results of this fascination with the problematics of language has been the excessive attention paid to writing congenial to the theory and practice of structuralism. It has led as well to a misreading of the distinct and unique intentions of current writing. Another and useful example of this tendency is the article by Gore Vidal, "American Plastic: The Matter of Fiction," in *Matters of Fact and Fiction* (New York: Vintage, 1978), pp. 99–126.

18. See Mendelson's discussion comparing Pynchon's ideas about language with those implicit in Joyce's *Ulysses*, in "Gravity's Encyclopedia." Readers of Pynchon will also be interested in the article by Thomas G. Winner, "Problems of Alphabetic Reform among the Turkic Peoples of Soviet Central Asia, 1920–41," *Slavonic and East European Review*, 31, no. 76 (December, 1952), 133–47. Mendelson uncovered this source and discusses it in his article on *Gravity's Rainbow*.

19. I think this is the major source of Pynchon's popularity. People feel less alienated when they read his books because they share in the community his books identify. This is not a community felt or understood by all readers, however.

Bibliography

Adams, Henry. *The Education of Henry Adams.* New York: Modern Library, 1931.
———. *The Degradation of the Democratic Dogma.* New York: Macmillan, 1919.
Arnheim, Rudolf. *Entropy and Art: An Essay on Disorder and Order.* Berkeley: University of California Press, 1971.
Barnett, Lincoln. *The Universe and Dr. Einstein.* New York: Bantam Books, 1957.
Barth, John. *Lost in the Funhouse.* Garden City, N.Y.: Doubleday, 1968.
———. "The Literature of Replenishment," *The Atlantic,* 245, no. 1 (January, 1980), 65–71.
Beal, M. F. *Amazon One.* Boston: Little, Brown, 1975.
Bellow, Saul. *Mr. Sammler's Planet.* Greenwich, Conn.: Fawcett Publications, 1970.
Berthoff, Warner. *A Literature without Qualities.* Berkeley: University of California Press, 1979.
Booth, Wayne. *The Rhetoric of Fiction.* Chicago: University of Chicago Press, 1961.
Bourne, Randolph. *War and the Intellectuals.* Ed. and intro. by Carl Resek. New York: Harper Torchbooks, 1964.
Boyer, Carl. *The Rainbow: From Myth to Mathematics.* New York: T. Yoseloff, 1959.
Bridgman, P. W. "The New Vision of Science." *Harper's Magazine,* 158 (March, 1929), 443–51.
Bronowski, Jacob. *The Ascent of Man.* Boston: Little, Brown, 1973.
Burroughs, William S. *Naked Lunch.* New York: Grove Press, 1959.
Chase, Richard. *The American Novel and Its Tradition.* Garden City, N.Y.: Doubleday, 1957.
Clarke, R. D. "An Application of the Poisson Distribution." *Journal of the Institute of Actuaries,* 72 (1946), 481.
Collier, Basil. *The Battle of the V-Weapons: 1944–45.* New York: William Morrow, 1965.

Cowart, David. "Pynchon's *The Crying of Lot 49* and the Paintings of Remedios Varo." *Critique,* 18, no. 3 (1977) 19–26.

Dampier, Sir William Cecil. *A History of Science.* 4th ed. Cambridge: Cambridge University Press, 1966.

Davidson, Gustav. *A Dictionary of Angels.* New York: Free Press, 1967.

Davis, Franklin M., Jr. *Come as a Conqueror: The United States Army's Occupation of Germany: 1945–49.* New York: Macmillan, 1967.

Dirac, P. A. M. "The Evolution of the Physicist's Picture of Nature." *Scientific American,* 208, no. 5 (May, 1963), 45–53.

Dornberger, Walter. *V-2.* Trans. James Cleugh and Geoffrey Halliday. New York: Viking Press, 1958.

Eddington, A. S. *Space, Time and Gravitation: An Outline of the General Relativity Theory.* Cambridge: Cambridge University Press, 1921.

The Egyptian Book of the Dead. Ed. Sir E. A. Budge. 3 vols. in 1. New York: Barnes & Noble, 1969.

Eliade, Mircea. *The Myth of the Eternal Return.* Trans. Willard R. Trask. London: Routledge & Kegan Paul, 1955.

———. *The Sacred and the Profane.* Trans. Willard R. Trask. New York: Harcourt, Brace & World, 1959.

Everson, William K. *The Bad Guys: A Pictorial History of the Movie Villain.* New York: Citadel Press, 1964.

Fariña, Richard. *Been Down So Long It Looks Like Up to Me.* New York: Random House, 1966.

Feller, William. *An Introduction to Probability Theory and Its Applications.* Vol. 1. New York: John Wiley, 1957.

Fiedler, Leslie. *Love and Death in the American Novel.* New York: Stein & Day, 1966.

Forster, E. M. *Aspects of the Novel.* New York: Harcourt, Brace & World, 1955.

Frazer, Sir James George. *The New Golden Bough.* Ed. Theodor H. Gaster. New York: Criterion Books, 1964.

Friedrich, Otto. *Before the Deluge: A Portrait of Berlin in the 1920's.* New York: Harper & Row, 1972.

Fuller, Buckminster. "Vertical Is to Live—Horizontal Is to Die." *American Scholar,* 39, no. 1 (Winter, 1969–70), 27–47.

Fussell, Paul. *The Great War and Modern Memory.* New York: Oxford University Press, 1975.

Goldner, Orville, and George E. Turner. *The Making of King Kong.* New York: Barnes & Noble, 1975.

Greenberg, Alvin. "The Underground Woman: An Excursion into the V-ness of Thomas Pynchon." *Chelsea,* 27 (1969), 58–65.

Hafen, Le Roy R. *The Overland Mail 1849–69.* Cleveland: A. H. Clark, 1926.

Harburg, E. Y. "Over the Rainbow." New York: Leo Feist, Inc., 1967.

Heisenberg, Werner. *Physics and Beyond.* New York: Harper & Row, 1971.

Herrigel, Eugen. *Zen in the Art of Archery*. Trans. R. F. C. Hull. New York: Vintage Books, 1953.

Hertzberg, Hendrik, and David C. K. McClelland. "Paranoia." *Harper's Magazine*, 248 (June, 1974), 51–54.

Hoffman, Frederick, Jr. "The Questing Comedian: Thomas Pynchon's *V.*" *Critique*, 6, no. 3 (Winter, 1963–64), 174–77.

Huzel, Dieter K. *Peenemünde to Canaveral*. Englewood Cliffs, N.J.: Prentice-Hall, 1962.

Hyman, Stanley Edgar. "The Goddess and the Schlemihl." *New Leader*, 46 (Mar. 18, 1963), 22–23.

Introduction to Aristotle. Ed. Richard McKeon. New York: Modern Library, 1947.

James, Henry. *The Art of the Novel*. Ed. R. P. Blackmur. New York: Scribner's, 1947.

Jennings, Hargrave. *The Rosicrucians*. London: Routledge & Kegan Paul, 1921.

Jonas, Hans. *The Gnostic Religion*. Boston: Beacon Press, 1958.

Jones, Howard Mumford. *O Strange New World*. New York: Viking Press, 1964.

Jung, C. G. *The Collected Works*. Trans. R. F. C. Hull. Princeton, N.J.: Princeton University Press, 1954–72.

———. "Psychological Commentary." In *The Tibetan Book of the Dead*. Ed. W. Y. Evans-Wentz. New York: Oxford University Paperback, 1960.

Koestler, Arthur. *The Roots of Coincidence*. New York: Random House, 1972.

Kracauer, Siegfried. *From Caligari to Hitler: A Psychological History of the German Film*. Princeton, N.J.: Princeton University Press, 1971.

Levi-Strauss, Claude. *Triste Tropiques*. Trans. John and Doreen Weightman. New York: Atheneum, 1975.

Ley, Willy. *Rockets, Missiles and Space Travel*. New York: Viking Press, 1958.

Luttig, Hendrik Gerhardus. *The Religious System and Social Organization of the Herero*. Utrecht, 1933.

Machiavelli. *The Prince*. Trans. George Bull. Penguin Books, 1961.

Mailer, Norman. *The Armies of the Night*. New York: New American Library, 1968.

Mangel, Anne. "Maxwell's Demon, Entropy, Information: *The Crying of Lot 49.*" In *Mindful Pleasures: Essays on Thomas Pynchon*. Ed. George Levine and David Leverenz. Boston: Little, Brown, 1976.

Matthiessen, Peter. *At Play in the Fields of the Lord*. New York: Random House, 1965.

McGovern, James. *Crossbow and Overcast*. New York: William Morrow, 1964.

McIntyre, Ruth A. *William Pynchon: Merchant and Colonizer 1590–1662*. Springfield, Mass.: Connecticut Valley Historical Museum, 1961.

McLuhan, Marshall. *Understanding Media: The Extensions of Man.* 2d ed. New York: New American Library, 1964.

Mendelson, Edward. "Gravity's Encyclopedia." In *Mindful Pleasures: Essays on Thomas Pynchon.* Ed. George Levine and David Leverenz. Boston: Little, Brown, 1976.

———. "The Sacred, the Profane and *The Crying of Lot 49.*" In *Pynchon: A Collection of Critical Essays.* Ed. Edward Mendelson. Englewood Cliffs, N.J.: Prentice-Hall, 1978.

Miller, Henry. *Tropic of Cancer.* New York: Ballantine Books, 1973.

Mindful Pleasures: Essays on Thomas Pynchon. Ed. George Levine and David Leverenz. Boston: Little, Brown, 1976.

"Nosepicking Contests." *Time,* 87 (May 6, 1966), 109–10.

Ozier, Lance. "The Calculus of Transformation: More Mathematical Imagery in *Gravity's Rainbow.*" *Twentieth Century Literature,* 21, no. 2 (May, 1975), 193–210.

Pavlov, I. P. *Conditioned Reflexes and Psychiatry.* Trans. Horsley Gantt. New York: International Publisher Co., 1941.

———. *Conditioned Reflexes: An Investigation of the Physiological Activity of the Cerebral Cortex.* Trans. G. V. Anrep. New York: Oxford University Press, 1927.

Pierce, J. R. *Symbols, Signals and Noise: The Nature and Process of Communication.* New York: Harper & Row, 1961.

Plater, William. *The Grim Phoenix.* Bloomington: Indiana University Press, 1978.

Poirier, Richard. "The Importance of Thomas Pynchon." In *Mindful Pleasures: Essays on Thomas Pynchon.* Ed. George Levine and David Leverenz. Boston: Little, Brown, 1976.

Puttkammer, Ernst W. *The Princes of Thurn and Taxis.* Chicago: Chicago Literary Club, 1938.

Pynchon: A Collection of Critical Essays. Ed. Edward Mendelson. Englewood Cliffs, N.J.: Prentice-Hall, 1978.

Pynchon, Thomas. *The Crying of Lot 49.* New York: Bantam Books, 1966.

———. "Entropy." *Kenyon Review,* 22 (1960), 277–92.

———. *Gravity's Rainbow.* New York: Viking Press, 1973.

———. "Under the Rose." *The Noble Savage,* no. 3 (1961), 223–51.

———. *V.* New York: Bantam Books, 1963.

Pynchon, William. *The Meretorious Price of Our Redemption.* London, 1650.

Redfield, Robert, and Peter L. Hays. "Fugue as Structure in Pynchon's 'Entropy.'" *Pacific Coast Philology,* 12 (1977), 50–55.

Reed, Ishmael. *Mumbo Jumbo.* Garden City, N.Y.: Doubleday, 1972.

———. *Yellow Back Radio Broke-Down.* New York: Avon Books, 1969.

Remedios Varo. Mexico: Ediciones Era, 1969.

Rilke, Rainer Maria. *The Book of Hours.* Trans. A. L. Peck. London: Hogarth Press, 1961.

————. *Duino Elegies*. Trans. J. B. Leishman and Stephen Spender. New York: Norton Library, 1963.

————. *Sonnets to Orpheus*. Trans. M. D. Herter Norton. New York: Norton Library, 1962.

Robbins, Tom. *Even Cowgirls Get the Blues*. Boston: Houghton-Mifflin, 1976.

Rotha, Paul. *The Film Till Now*. New York: Funk & Wagnalls, 1949.

Russell, Charles. "The Vault of Language: Self-Reflective Artifice in Contemporary American Fiction." *Modern Fiction Studies*, 20, no. 3 (Autumn, 1974), 349–59.

Sanders, Scott. "Pynchon's Paranoid History." In *Mindful Pleasures: Essays on Thomas Pynchon*. Ed. George Levine and David Leverenz. Boston: Little, Brown, 1976.

Schickel, Richard. "Paranoia at Full Cry." *World*, 2, no. 8 (Apr. 10, 1973), 43–44.

Scholem, Gershom G. *On the Kabbalah and Its Symbolism*. Trans. Ralph Manheim. New York: Schocken Books, 1965.

Shirer, William L. *Berlin Diary*. New York: Alfred A. Knopf, 1941.

Siegel, Mark. *Creative Paranoia in Gravity's Rainbow*. New York: Kennikat Press, 1978.

Slade, Joseph. "Escaping Rationalization: Options for the Self in *Gravity's Rainbow*." *Critique*, 18, no. 3 (1977), 27–38.

————. *Thomas Pynchon*. New York: Warner Paperback Library, 1974.

Thackeray, William Makepeace. *Vanity Fair*. Boston: Houghton-Mifflin, 1963.

Todorov, Tzvetan. *The Fantastic*. Trans. Richard Howard. Cleveland: Press of Case Western Reserve University, 1973.

Tolstoi, Leo. *War and Peace*. New York: New American Library, 1968.

Trent, William P. *A History of American Literature, 1607–1865*. New York: D. Appleton, 1903.

Van Nostrand's Scientific Encyclopedia. New York: D. Van Nostrand, 1947.

Vidal, Gore. *Matters of Fact and Fiction*. New York: Vintage Books, 1978.

Waite, Arthur E. *The Holy Kabbalah*. New Hyde Park, N.Y.: University Books, 1959.

————. *Pictorial Key to the Tarot*. New Hyde Park, N.Y.: University Books, 1959.

Weber, Max. *From Max Weber: Essays in Sociology*. Trans. and ed. H. H. Gerth and C. Wright Mills. New York: Oxford University Press, 1946.

————. *The Theory of Social and Economic Organization*. Trans. A. M. Henderson and Talcott Parsons. New York: Oxford University Press, 1947.

Weisskopf, Victor. *Knowledge and Wonder*. Garden City, N.Y.: Doubleday, 1966.

Whitehead, Alfred North. *Science and the Modern World*. New York: Free Press, 1967.

Wiener, Norbert. *The Human Use of Human Beings: Cybernetics and Society.* New York: Avon Books, 1967.

Winner, Thomas G. "Problems of Alphabetic Reform among the Turkic Peoples of Soviet Central Asia, 1920–41." *Slavonic and East European Review,* 31, no. 76 (December, 1952), 133–47.

Winston, Mathew. "The Quest for Pynchon." In *Mindful Pleasures: Essays on Thomas Pynchon.* Ed. George Levine and David Leverenz. Boston: Little, Brown, 1976.

Wittgenstein, Ludwig. *Tractatus Logico-Philosophicus.* Trans. D. F. Pears and B. F. McGuinness. London: Routledge & Kegan Paul, 1961.

Yates, Francis A. *Giordano Bruno and the Hermetic Tradition.* Chicago: University of Chicago Press, 1964.

———. *The Theatre of the World.* Chicago: University of Chicago Press, 1969.

Index

Accident, 7, 8; and Fortune, 12, 19n8;
and design, 104–12. See also
Determinism
Achtfaden, Horst, 77, 89
Adams, Henry, 3, 4, 22, 23, 76, 119,
120
Ambiguity, 3–20 passim; American
tradition, 146–49; in concepts of
entropy, 21–42 passim; and concept
of "integration," 55–57, 70–73; in
reading Pynchon, 3–4, 13–14,
16–18, 19, 104–38; of facts, 31,
112–23 passim; intentional creation
of, 103–38; of metaphor, 38, 106–7;
in Oedipa's understanding, 21–42;
in presentation of paranoia, 77,
90–91; of the "real present," 12–13,
19; of the Situation, 12, 5–19
passim, 103–23 passim;
surrounding V., 16; and values,
123–36. See also Uncertainty
Aristotle, 46, 50, 52
Aubade, 23

Bad Priest, 79
Barth, John, 149–50, 154n15
Beal, M. F., 139, 152n2
Bianca, 44
Bland, Lyle, 50, 69–70, 100–101
Blicero, Captain Dominus, 44, 63, 66,
126, 131. See also Weissmann
Bloat, Teddy, 17, 73, 131
Blobadjian, Igor, 50, 98
Bodine, Seaman "Pig," 10, 19, 60–61,
73, 95, 96, 134, 142
Boethius, 9

Bohr, Niels, 121
Bongo-Shaftesbury, 79
Borgesius, Katje, 57, 63, 127, 131,
136
Bortz, Emory, 34
Borkin, Joseph, 102n20
Bourne, Randolph, 94
Boyer, Carl, 48
Bridgman, P. W., 117
Bronowski, Jacob, 121
Bummer, Säure, 7, 134–35
Bureaucracy, 51, 58–63 passim; and
charisma, 58, 59; and love, 61–63.
See also Weber, Max
Burroughs, William S., 140, 143

Callisto, 23–24, 107, 111
Carruthers-Pillow, 111
Cause-and-effect, 7, 8; history, 15, 76,
98; and Pavlov's brain mechanics,
50, 90–94
Chance. See Accident; Design;
Determinism
Charisma, 57–63 passim
Chemistry. See Continuity
the Child: in Advent imagery, 66–67;
in Hansel and Gretel, 63–65; as
object, 44; in Pynchon's writing,
43–45, 63–65; in The Wizard of Oz,
43, 45, 64
Chilkes, Maudie, 136
Clarke, R. D., 108–9
Clemens, Samuel, 147
Closed system. See Entropy
Cohen, Genghis, 38, 40,
128

Communications: and absence of community, 41; as extensions of man, 25, 28; in study of society, 28–29. *See also* Information; McLuhan, Marshall; Wiener, Norbert

Conrad, Joseph, 95, 148

Contingency: of the Situation, 14, 7–20 *passim. See also* Accident; Situation

Continuity: and abstraction, 10–16 *passim*; and calculus, 46; chemical, 10, 88, 97–101; chosen, 47; of dream material, 51; of film, 43–49; of love, 62; of metaphor, 37, 40; of Pynchon's voice, 123–36 *passim*; of the Self, 55, 70–73; of space and time, 4, 8, 11

Control: economic, 94–97; illusion of, 51, 69; and rationalization of experience, 63–66. *See also* Bureaucracy; Weber, Max

Coover, Robert, 149

Cross-purposes: in formation of the Situation, 9–13. *See also* Situation

The Crying of Lot 49, 11–12, 13, 44, 77, 98, 126, 128, 129, 142, 146, 147, 148, 149; and ambiguity of experience, 21–42 *passim*; and myth of Narcissus, 25–26; and stylistic ambiguity, 104–19 *passim*

Counterforce, 59–61

Design, 7, 8, 104–12

Determinism, 3, 8–20 *passim*, 10; and freedom, 45–46, 104–12 *passim*; imagery of, 50–51; and Pavlov's ideas, 90, 92–93

Dodson-Truck, Nora, 97

Dodson-Truck, Sir Stephen, 55

Dornberger, Walter, 47

Driblette, Randy, 33, 34

Dubnietna, 122

Dupiro, 9

Eddington, Sir Arthur, 8–9

The Education of Henry Adams. See Adams, Henry

The Egyptian Book of the Dead, 35

Eigenvalue, Dudley, 46

Einstein, Albert, 8, 127

Eliade, Mircea, 83–88 *passim*, 88, 105, 108

Eliot, Thomas Stearns, 44, 139

Ellison, Ralph, 138n24, 147

Emerson, Ralph Waldo, 112

"Entropy," 5, 6, 22–24, 107, 111

Entropy, 5–20 *passim*; and closed systems, 22–27; and information, 21, 27–31; as metaphor of decline, 5, 6

Enzian, Oberst, 14–15, 59, 65, 68, 89, 99, 131, 134; and Return, 84–88

Erdmann, Margherita, 7, 44

Eventyr, Carroll, 69

Facts. *See* Ambiguity

Faggio Guard, 39, 40

Fahringer, 92, 123

Fallopian, Mike, 38

Fariña, Richard, 139–41 *passim*

Faulkner, William, 147

Feedback, 5, 18–19, 28; and information, 28–42 *passim*

Feel, Osbie, 59, 131

Feldspath, Roland, 50, 54, 69, 92, 93

Feller, William, 108–9

Fibel, Bert, 123

Fielding, Henry, 130, 131

Film, 43–49

Flaum, 123

Foppl, 46, 81

Fowles, John, 149

Frazer, Sir James, 71, 144

Free will. *See* Determinism

Garland, Judy, 43

Gerfaut, 44

Gibbs, Willard, 22

Gödel, Kurt, 50

Godolphin, Hugh, 13, 46

Gottfried, 44, 63, 65–66, 86, 87, 99, 129–30, 142

Gravity, 49, 73, 100–101

Gravity's Rainbow, 3, 7, 10, 11, 13, 15, 43–75 *passim*, 77, 107, 114, 139–54 *passim*; and film, 43–49; and history, 83–101 *passim*; and Orphic narration, 123–36; and stylistic ambiguity, 108–12

Grigori, the octopus, 51, 89, 127, 142

Gwenhidwy, Thomas, 88–89, 93

Hansel and Gretel, 63–65
Harvitz, Esther, 128
Hawthorne, Nathaniel, 129, 146
Heisenberg, Werner, 50, 96, 117, 121
Hereros, 14, 83–88. *See also* Enzian
Hertzberg, Hendrik, 90
l'Heuremaudit, Mélanie, 44
Hilarius, Dr., 77
History: cause-and-effect, 15, 76, 98; and design of *V.*, 16–17; economic basis, 94–97; and entropy, 22; and the Hereros, 83–88; and randomness, 110; and revelation, 32–33; and search for meaning, 77–82; understood statistically, 14–15, 84
The Human Use of Human Beings, 5. *See also* Wiener, Norbert

Imipolex G, 48, 99
Information: and entropy, 21, 27–31; and revelation, 31–34; subject to decay, 38–40
Integration: ambiguity of, 55, 70–73; and fragmentation, 70; of love, 61–63; mandala symbol of, 17, 52–55; of the Rocket, 55–57
Inverarity, Pierce, 19, 25, 26–27, 33, 113

Jaguar, Tony, 35
James, Henry, 112–13, 147
Jamf, Lazlo, 44, 71, 144
Janet, Pierre, 90–93 *passim*
Jeremy, the Beaver, 61
Joyce, James, 139
Jung, Carl, 35, 49–57 *passim*, 65, 73

Kekulé von Stradowitz, Friedrich, 51, 52, 99–100, 143
King Kong, 57, 95
Kirghiz Light, 54, 151
Koestler, Arthur, 117
Koteks, Stanley, 21, 27
Krypton, Albert, 49

Lang, Fritz, 47
Leibnitz, Gottfried, 46
Levi-Strauss, Claude, 54
Ley, Willy, 47
"Lowlands," 6
Luttig, Hendrik Gerhardus, 85–87

Maas, Mucho, 25, 40, 77, 113, 149
Maas, Oedipa, 11–12, 16, 18, 19, 21–42 *passim*, 44, 45, 61, 71, 72, 77, 79, 80, 104, 105, 113–23 *passim*, 128, 129, 147, 149, 150
McClelland, David, 90
Machiavelli, Niccolò, 12
McLuhan, Marshall, 24–26, 27, 39–41 *passim*
Magda, 7
Maijstral, Fausto, 9, 69, 79, 106, 121, 147
Mailer, Norman, 61
Malcolm X, 63, 95, 141, 144
Mandalas, 14, 17, 51–57. *See also* Integration
Manganese, 9
Mara, 16–17
Marvy, Major Duane, 94
Matthiessen, Peter, 140, 145–46
Maxwell, Clerk, 27
Maxwell's Demon, 27–28, 29, 30
Mehemet, 16–17
Melville, Herman, 48, 118–20, 146, 147
Metaphor, 23, 29–30, 31, 33, 37, 38, 82, 106–7
Metzger, 35, 45, 113
Mexico, Roger, 14, 15, 17, 50, 54, 59, 60, 61–62, 64, 66–67, 69, 91, 92, 95, 97, 108, 110, 127, 131, 135, 136
Miller, Henry, 5
Mizzi, 9
Moby-Dick, 48, 114
Moldweorp, 78, 79
Mondaugen, Kurt, 46, 81, 82, 123; electro-mysticism of, 70–73
Mossmoon, Clive, 136
Mucker-Maffick, Tantivy, 77, 127
Mulligan, Meatball, 23–24, 107, 111

Narcissus myth, 25–26, 31
Närrisch, Klaus, 71, 123
Nefastis, John, 29, 30, 39, 114

Newton, Sir Isaac, 7, 48, 121
Niccolò, 115
Nixon, Richard M., 148

Oberth, Hermann, 47
Oedipus, 149
Ölsch, Etzel, 57
Ombindi, Josef, 85
Ortega y Gasset, José, 78
Orukambe, Andreas, 52–53
"Over the Rainbow," 45
Owlglass, Rachel, 128, 133

Paranoia, 34, 41, 45, 76–77, 88–101
    passim; Pavlov's mechanical
    explanation of, 90–94
Pavlov, Ivan P., 73, 88, 90–94 passim
Pierce, J. R., 29, 30
Pinguid records, 32–33
Pinocchio, 45
Planck, Max, 50
Poe, Edgar Allan, 147
Pointsman, Edward, 15, 44, 50, 63,
    88–94 passim, 110, 126, 128–29,
    136
Poisson: equation, 15; distribution,
    108–10, 137
Pokler, Franz, 44, 47, 64–65, 68, 70,
    123, 126, 132
Pokler, Ilse, 44, 47, 64, 70
Pokler, Leni, 18, 44, 47, 54, 64, 70,
    92
Porpentine, 78, 79
Prentice, Pirate, 50, 60, 73, 80, 108,
    131
Puttkammer, Ernst, 115–16
Pynchon, Thomas, 43, 148–49. See
    also names of individual characters
    and works

Qulan, Džaqyp, 53, 151, 152

Rathenau, Walter, 10, 50, 59, 98
Rebecca, 134
Reed, Ishmael, 139, 140, 141–45
    passim
Revelation. See Information
Rilke, Rainer Maria, 14, 20n10, 50,
    72–73
Robbins, Tom, 139, 141, 142, 143

the Rocket, 14–15, 55, 65–66, 68, 73,
    85, 98, 100–101, 122–23
Rooney, Mickey, 43

Sachsa, Peter, 70
Scammony, Sir Marcus, 136
Schlabone, Gustav, 134–35
Schnorp, 59, 95
Schoenmaker, Shale, 12, 128
Second Law of Thermodynamics, 22.
    See also Entropy
the Self, 49, 50, 55–57, 70–73,
    74–75n13
Silvernail, Webley, 68, 99, 101
the Situation, 5–20 passim, 70, 76,
    88, 96, 97, 123, 124; ambiguity of,
    103–23 passim; composed of
    cross-purposes, 9–13; and the "real
    present," 11–13
Slothrop, Tyrone, 7, 10, 13–14, 17, 18,
    19, 43, 44, 49, 51, 58, 59, 60, 63, 68,
    70–73, 75n19, 84, 89, 90, 91, 93, 94,
    95, 99, 108, 123–32 passim, 135,
    136, 142, 145–46, 148, 150
Smith, Adam, 94–95
Spectro, Kevin, 92, 93
Sphere, McClintic, 19
Squalidozzi, Francisco, 59
Squamuglia, Duke of, 40
Stencil, Herbert, 11, 13, 16, 18, 19, 40,
    77, 78–80, 116, 150
Stencil, Sidney, 5, 6, 8, 10, 16–17, 41,
    69, 76, 78, 88, 96, 97, 111, 123, 124,
    147
Swanlake, Jessica, 15, 17, 59, 61–62,
    64, 66–67, 68, 97, 127, 136

Tchitcherine, Old, 151
Tchitcherine, Vaslav, 53, 61, 62–63,
    69, 70, 96, 131, 151–52
Temple, Shirley, 43, 44
Thackeray, Makepeace, 131, 135, 136
Thermodynamics. See Entropy
Thoth, Mr., 32
Thoth (Egyptian god), 35
Thurn and Taxis, 114–16
Tibetan Book of the Dead, 35
Todorov, Tzvetan, 106, 108
Tolstoi, Leo, 76
Tripping, Geli, 61, 62–63, 70, 131, 135

Tristero, 14, 40, 80, 98, 114, 115;
as alternative, 32; relation to
Oedipa, 36–37, 38; and revelation,
34–42
Tropic of Cancer, 5–6

Uncertainty, 3, 4, 3–20 *passim*, 34,
50, 63–66, 96, 104–23 *passim. See
also* Ambiguity
Understanding Media, 24–26, 41. *See
also* McLuhan, Marshall
"Under the Rose," 6, 77–79
Utgarthaloki, Stefan, 61, 95, 142

V., 16–17, 79–80
V., 5–20 *passim*, 46, 54, 76, 78–82,
88, 106, 111–12, 121–22, 123, 124,
126, 128, 133, 147, 148
Varo, Remedios, 31
Von Braun, Werner, 117
Von Göll, Gerhardt, 54
Von Trotha, General Lothar, 81–82,
84

Weber, Max, 50, 57–63, 73, 78, 89,
134
Weichensteller, 123
Weisskopf, Victor, 100
Weissmann, Lieutenant, 68, 81–82,
84, 86, 87, 123, 134, 136, 148. *See
also* Blicero, Captain Dominus
Wharfinger, 115
"When You Wish upon a Star," 45
Whitehead, Alfred North, 120
Wiener, Norbert, 5, 7, 18, 22–23, 39
Wigglesworth, Brenda, 133
Wimpe, 69, 96
Wittgenstein, Ludwig, 81–82, 119, 120
Wizard of Oz, 43, 45, 49, 64
Wordsworth, William, 97, 123
Wren, Victoria, 79
Wuxtry-Wuxtry, Mickey, 71

Yates, Francis, 52

Zeno's paradox, 46
Zhlubb, Richard M., 73, 126, 142